Drayton Hall: Preliminary Archaeological

Investigation at a Low Country Plantation

DRAYTON HALL
Preliminary Archaeological Investigation at a Low Country Plantation

By Lynne G. Lewis

PUBLISHED FOR
NATIONAL TRUST FOR HISTORIC PRESERVATION
BY THE UNIVERSITY PRESS OF VIRGINIA
CHARLOTTESVILLE

Drayton Hall: Preliminary Archaeological Investigation at a Low Country
Plantation is one of a series of research reports from the Office of
Historic Properties of the National Trust for Historic Preservation.
These reports present studies pertaining to various aspects of preser-
vation and research on the structures, sites and collections maintained
by the National Trust.

The National Trust for Historic Preservation, chartered by Congress in 1949,
is the only private, nonprofit organization with the responsibility to
encourage public participation in the preservation of sites, buildings and
objects significant in American history and culture. Support is provided
by membership dues, endowment funds and contributions and by matching
grants from federal agencies, including the U.S. Department of the Interior,
**Heritage Conservation and Recreation Service, under provisions of the
National Historic Preservation Act of 1966.**

THE PRESERVATION PRESS
National Trust for Historic Preservation
740-748 Jackson Place, N.W.
Washington, D.C.   20006

Historic American Buildings Survey measured drawing of Drayton Hall.

CONTENTS

Figures, continued

Figures, continued

Located on the Ashley River some 12 miles northwest of Charleston, S.C., Drayton Hall is the oldest and the finest surviving example of early Georgian architecture in the South. The house was constructed between 1738 and 1742, only 70 years after the founding of the first permanent settlement by Europeans in Carolina.

Thomas Drayton, the first of his family to settle in the colony, was not among the original settlers who arrived in 1670. Like many of their neighbors, the Draytons had emigrated from England to Barbados first and then to Carolina. Before 1700, however, Thomas Drayton had located his family at Magnolia Plantation on the Ashley River.

Thomas Drayton's son, the Hon. John Drayton, was a member of His Majesty's Council, advisors to the royal governor. In 1738 John Drayton acquired land just south of his father's plantation and construction of Drayton Hall was apparently started soon thereafter. John Drayton named his new residence after the family estate in Northamptonshire, which had been the ancestral seat of the Draytons since their arrival in England with William the Conqueror in 1066. John Drayton was not yet 30 when he moved his family into their new house; while the exact date of the move is unknown, the eldest surviving son of John's second marriage, William Henry, was born at Drayton Hall on September 20, 1742. From that time until 1974--through seven consecutive generations-- the estate remained in the Drayton family.

Drayton Hall was a product of the plantation system that brought wealth, culture and grandeur to the South Carolina low country. From his estate John Drayton supervised the operation of nearly a score of plantations throughout the region in the colonial period.

During the American Revolution the builder of Drayton Hall died and the estate passed in turn to his son, his grandson and his great-grandson; all three were named Charles and all three were physicians. The fourth Charles Drayton, great-great-grandson of the builder, was a businessman. He acquired Drayton Hall on the eve of the War Between the States and thus was witness to the abrupt ending of the plantation system. Drayton Hall, the splendid structure that symbolized the best of the plantation way of life, survived the war. Following the example of Gen. William T. Sherman in the central midlands of South Carolina, local Union troops systematically burned the plantation houses along the Ashley River. Since Charles was a minor, the plantation was managed by his uncle, Dr. John Drayton, who signaled that the house was being used for smallpox victims. Whether this was a ruse or the house was actually being used as a hospital is uncertain, but it worked, and Drayton Hall alone, of all the plantations on the Ashley, survived.

The bleak days of Reconstruction changed the house only slightly, with some damage in the stairhall. During the 1870s, the roof had to be replaced after water had destroyed the plaster ceilings on the second floor and caused the installation of the present board ceilings. The two-story flanking dependency to the north was destroyed by the great earthquake of 1886, and the flanking dependency to the south was razed in the 1890s after damage from a hurricane. The dwelling has never had plumbing, gas lights, electricity or central heating systems installed.

Eventually, the Drayton family stopped using the plantation house except for a few weeks each year during the spring and fall. By the mid-20th century it was obvious that the family that had created, loved and cared for this architectural masterpiece would have to find another owner to insure its survival.

In 1973 the National Trust for Historic Preservation and the Historic Charleston Foundation took an option on the property. By late 1974, funds for the purchase of the estate had been raised in a joint effort by the two organizations and Drayton Hall, along with 610 acres, was acquired. The Historic Charleston Foundation raised about half the amount necessary for purchase of the property. The remainder came from National Trust funds and a matching grant from the National Park Service, U.S. Department of the Interior. With the assistance of funds from the Bureau of Outdoor Recreation, U.S. Department of the Interior, 485 acres subsequently were purchased by South Carolina to be administered by the state Department of Parks, Recreation and Tourism.

The acquisition of Drayton Hall was accomplished by a unique tripartite arrangement involving the National Trust, the Historic Charleston Foundation and the state of South Carolina, which will see that the entire property is developed as a single entity. This cooperative arrangement represents a new and interesting venture in historic preservation efforts. An advisory body, the Drayton Hall Council, has equal representation from the three organizations and an ex officio representative of the Drayton family.

Both flankers and all but two dependencies have disappeared from the property. Except for what can be seen in a few late 19th-century photographs, little is known about these structures, so the first research project undertaken was archaeological. In 1974 the National Trust assigned Lynn G. Lewis, Trust historical archaeologist, to Drayton Hall and this publication is the result of her investigation of the property.

In late 1975 and early 1976, a historical architect and an architectural historian were hired, with the assistance of matching grants from the National Park Service, to study Drayton Hall--the house, other physical remains and all available documents.

The information revealed by the historical research shed light on many aspects of the archaeological work and provided confirmation of certain hypotheses formulated in the course of the excavations, as the report explains. Identification of physical remains, both excavated and found in the house, was done more quickly and with greater accuracy by having these several areas of expertise available on the site concurrently.

This report, along with the forthcoming reports of the historical architect and the architectural historian, will provide important contributions to the master planning and interpretation of Drayton Hall.

For 21 months, Lynne G. Lewis planned and carried out excavations at Drayton Hall. For much of this time, she also served as the National Trust agent for the property. Her experience and knowledge of what transpired plus her willingness to share and advise will always be much appreciated by the first administrator of the property.

Dennis T. Lawson, administrator
Drayton Hall

ACKNOWLEDGMENTS

During the 18 months spent at Drayton Hall numerous people helped with the
planning and execution of this project. Dennis W. Basler, field assistant,
was of enormous help in the initial stages of planning and surveying, as well
as in the actual excavations. Senior excavator Barbara L. Watts was of
invaluable assistance, especially during those periods when I had to be away
from the property. Amy E. Bennett, also senior excavator, provided humor and
hard work when the pressures were the greatest and her photography helped
greatly to bring the project to a successful conclusion. Although the crew
was never larger than four at one time, I must thank the several persons who
participated over the course of the 18 months: Charles J. Hasbrouck, Suzanne
Drone, Maggi Elliott, Robert Bacon, Bridget G. Brennan, John S. Antalis and
David A. Auten, our very own nature lad, who was responsible for capturing
the numerous snakes, lizards, toads, alligators and other wild creatures that
frequently crossed the diggings. Robert L. Gaskin, groundsman, deserves
special commendation for his keen eyesight, which produced numerous artifacts
and sites that might otherwise have been missed.

Charles E. Chase, historical architect, and Kevin Murphy, architectural
historian for the Drayton Hall project, both willingly assisted in providing
insight into areas of Drayton Hall's history with which I was unfamiliar.
Dennis T. Lawson, property administrator, deserves a special note of thanks
for his patience, wit and forbearance.

Frances Edmunds, executive director of the Historic Charleston Foundation,
and Charles Duell, director of Middleton Place, both provided assistance and
advice without which the work would have been far more difficult. Robert L.
Stephenson, state archaeologist for South Carolina and director of the Institute of Archeology and Anthropology at the University of South Carolina, and
Stanley South, archaeologist at the institute, helped in providing advice and
local information. Andrew Johnson of the U.S. Soil Conservation Service, and
Wilbur Campbell, River Basin Water Shed planning geologist in Columbia, S.C.,
provided technical assistance in their areas of specialization.

To Raymond G. Cofield, Jr., who provided the pump necessary to empty the well,
who throughout the entire period was always helpful and encouraging and who
taught me more about the South Carolina low country than anyone else, this
work is respectfully dedicated.

PRELIMINARY RESEARCH

The archaeological investigation of the Drayton Hall plantation was begun in February 1975 with the assistance of a National Park Service matching grant. When the National Trust for Historic Preservation acquired the Drayton Hall property in December 1974, it was determined that full-scale archaeological, architectural and historical research would be undertaken before the prepara- tion of a master plan for the property and before public visiting began.

The architectural historian joined the project in February 1976. Prior to that time research into the history of the property in order to obtain whatever information was available regarding the layout of Drayton Hall and other plantations of the same period was undertaken. Although numerous published works on architecture, the South, South Carolina, Charleston and related topics were consulted, information on the Drayton Hall estate proved to be scarce. Drawings, photographs and descriptions of the main house are abundant, but most are of recent vintage and add little to the extant knowledge of the property history.

In addition to published sources, several documentary sources were consulted, including both the Geography and Maps Division and the Manuscripts Division of the Library of Congress. Beyond some sketchy family history, however, little information was obtained from these sources. It should be noted that the National Union Catalog of Manuscript Collections revealed that there are few collections of Drayton papers in public repositories. The largest body of papers, at the Historical Society of Pennsylvania, is mainly concerned with the Philadelphia branch of the family.

At the Charleston County Courthouse all wills, inventories and miscellaneous papers relating to the Drayton family from 1697 to 1840 were reviewed. The 1724 will and inventory of the effects of the first Thomas Drayton were found and a preliminary family tree was constructed (Appendix A), but information regarding the side of the family that owned Drayton Hall is almost nonexistent. An investigation of the land records at the Charleston County Courthouse produced only one plat of the property, dated 20 August 1884. This plat shows the boundaries of the property but does not designate any buildings. A c. 1850 survey of the Ashley River area recently acquired by the Historic Charleston Foundation shows Drayton Hall with the two flankers and a third outbuilding but no other details.

The material on the Drayton family and Drayton Hall found in the South Carolina State Archives at Columbia, S.C., produced no direct information regarding the physical layout of the property but did provide a record of house- hold items turned over to Rebecca Drayton by Charles Drayton dated 10 September 1783, and a bill of sale from John Drayton to Thomas Ladson for various household items, dated 26 August 1745 (Appendix B). In addition, two King's Grants of land to John Drayton were located. Both were grants of marshland adjoining Drayton Hall, one dating from 7 May 1762, for 61.5 acres, the

8

other dating from 20 April 1763, for 78 acres. Other land grants, both royal and state, were located, but these related to other members of the family and the majority of them referred to other parts of South Carolina.

In January 1976, the Drayton family donated a large collection of papers to the Historic Charleston Foundation, including the diaries of Charles Drayton dating from 1779 to 1820. Charles Drayton, the second owner of Drayton Hall, made numerous repairs, improvements and additions to the property, all of which were carefully noted in his diaries. Of particular interest were the references to the multitude of outbuildings, often with sketches, which showed that most of the structures were of simple wood construction on brick piers. Regrettably, however, Drayton did not indicate the location of any of the structures. As shown by the constant reference to new barns and "negroe barracks," these structures apparently were short lived. The type of construction used, the rampant overgrowth of any untended areas and the extensive strip-mining over much of the property, would make it virtually impossible to locate the buildings, as a visual survey over the land area surrounding the house confirmed. Only one of these once-numerous outbuildings at Drayton Hall is in evidence today--a small mid 18th-century brick building. Structures from later periods still standing are a barn, a small Victorian cottage dating from the late 19th century and a well from the 1930s. The main house originally was flanked by two smaller brick buildings, the foundation outlines of which are still visible, with the north* outline showing more clearly than the south. There are traces of cabins in the woods on the north and south sides of the main drive and two tumbled cabin ruins on the south. There is also evidence of a single structure west of the small pond on the land side of the house. The remains of a phosphate mining office and a phosphate reducing operation are evident along the riverbank. A chimney still stands to the north of the barn, and the ruins of an 18th-century orangery (fig. 1) are located along the riverbank in the northern section of the gardens. There is also a graveyard for blacks, in use as recently as 1964, to the north of the main drive.

Scattered throughout the property are various nonstructural remains, including several privy holes, small garbage dumps and liquor still holes. Many of these remains date from the late 19th and early 20th centuries; however, one dump on the northern edge of the lawn produced artifacts that date it from the last quarter of the 18th century. Unfortunately for archaeologists, the Ashley River flows swiftly by less than 150 yards from the main house and no doubt served as a convenient garbage disposal.

The remains of the phosphate-mining process are still apparent. The roadbed for a narrow-gauge railway that ran from the western end of the property to a bridge over the river and on to Charleston is still plainly visible in many areas, as are some of the bridge pilings and the office and refining areas mentioned earlier. Caches of pickax heads and miscellaneous mining

---

*The true north-south axis runs through the corners of the house, an orientation termed the "Indies Orientation," which was specified in The Laws of the Indies of 1573. For purposes of the excavation, the north line was shifted 43.7° west of north, i.e., the north-south axis was made perpendicular to the facades of the house. All written, photographic, grid and drawing references are made on this assumed axis; however, the topographical and overall site plan use the true north.

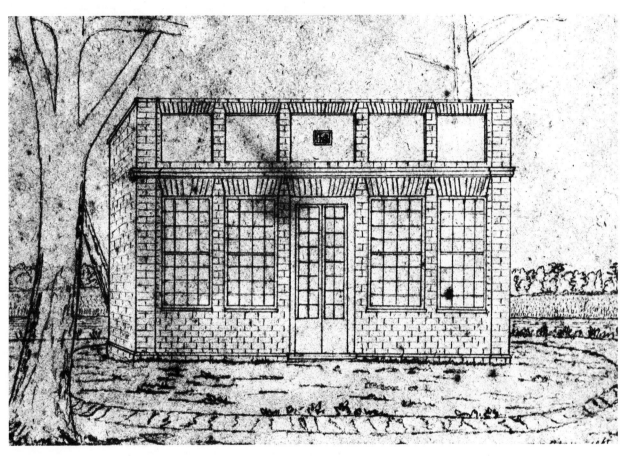

Figure 1: The orangery at Drayton Hall. (Courtesy of the Drayton family)

equipment and occasional rails can be found in the vicinity of the barn and railroad bed.

It was the goal of the preliminary archaeological investigations to locate as many sites as possible through a visual survey of the property, concentrating on the 125 acres owned by the National Trust. After completion of the survey, conducted largely during November and December 1974 while the archaeologist was on site acting as National Trust agent, excavations were begun in the area of the main house. The goals of the excavation were to determine the size, nature and construction of the flanker buildings; investigate the drive area to determine its original pattern; investigate the brick and stone paving used on the ground floor of the house; determine the original grade along the house; establish the way the main house and flankers were connected, if they were; and undertake other investigations as necessary or as time permitted. Areas that might be adversely affected by opening the property to the public were also studied. The original project was to run for six to nine months but was extended to 18 months due to bad weather and the great wealth of information retrieved.

One of the archaeological research goals was to determine the lifestyle of the occupants of Drayton Hall through analysis of the recovered materials. While a great deal has been written about 18th and 19th-century plantation life in the South, the specific types and uses of household items and tools have not often been delineated. Through the archaeological method, such things as garbage disposal, sanitation and travel patterns can be revealed. In many cases the archaeological remains not only supplement the historical and architectural record, but also add a dimension that the documents do not provide.

Stanley South, archaeologist at the Institute of Archaeology and Anthropology, University of South Carolina, states that "archaeologists should focus their efforts toward the discovery and explication of patterns of material culture" (South 1974:168-9), rather than merely cataloguing recovered artifacts. This concept has guided the work done at Drayton Hall. The information gained from the archaeological investigations there adds to the understanding of the pattern of life in low country South Carolina, augments the picture of plantation life both before and after the American Revolution and reflects the changes brought about by the rise and fall of the plantation system.

THE DRAYTON FAMILY

The Drayton family can be traced back as far as 1066, when Albrec DeVere (the original form of the Drayton name) arrived in England with William the Conqueror. In 1675 a branch of the family moved to the Barbados, and in 1678 Thomas Drayton sailed on the ship Mary to Carolina. Along the Ashley River, Thomas purchased the land known today as Magnolia Gardens and there established the South Carolina seat of the Drayton family. When Thomas died he left Magnolia to his eldest son, Thomas, and the neighboring land to his youngest son, John.

In 1738 John began construction of Drayton Hall and in 1742 his son William Henry was born there. The architect of Drayton Hall has not been identified, but his sophistication and knowledge of current architectural modes is apparent. He adhered closely to the English Palladian concept of design, and the overmantel in the first floor great hall is a close copy of one in Kent's Designs of Inigo Jones (1727). An example of the architect's sophistication is seen in the fact that the flanker buildings were set approximately two degrees off a line perpendicular to the main house. From a distance, the human eye corrects this offset--proving that the designer obviously knew how to use optical illusion to advantage. If the flankers had been placed perpendicular to the house, from a distance it would have appeared that they angled in toward the house.

From the time of construction until it was acquired by the National Trust in 1974, Drayton Hall never left the possession of the Drayton family. Remarkably, the main house never had central heating, plumbing or electricity installed, although it was inhabited until 1910 and used in the summer until 1969.

In pre-Revolutionary South Carolina the main cash crop was indigo; by the time of the Revolution, rice had begun to replace indigo in importance. However, according to a local botanist (Hastie, personal communication), the lower Ashley River was not a major rice-producing area, due to the brackish river water and the lack of any extensive uplands for reservoirs. The rice grown at Drayton Hall was probably sufficient to support the plantation population, but no more.

Support for this theory is provided by Charles Drayton's diaries and by the fact that the Draytons owned extensive acreage in other parts of South Carolina as well as in Canada, Kentucky and Georgia. In South Carolina they had plantations in Colleton County, on the Edisto River, in Berkeley County and in up-country South Carolina as well as a residence on Sullivan's Island and one in Charleston proper. The plantations produced the major cash crops (indigo, rice and cotton), while Drayton Hall served as the business management and country seat for the Drayton holdings; many of the crops were brought to Drayton Hall and distributed from there.

The Drayton family fortunes prospered until the Civil War and the collapse of the plantation system. Unlike other plantation houses on the Ashley River, Drayton Hall was not destroyed when Union troops passed through Charleston. During and immediately after the war the house occasionally was occupied by squatters (Providence [R.I.] Journal 1885) and suffered from neglect, but it was rescued from further deterioration in the late 1870s by the discovery of the utility of the large phosphate deposits in the area. The wealth accumulated during this period helped pay for much needed repair, including replacement of the slate roof with tin and the covering of the brick pediment with imbricated wooden shingles.

In the 20th century, use of the property declined to just a few weeks each year. In 1974, with the help of the Historic Charleston Foundation and with a matching grant from the National Park Service, U.S. Department of the Interior, the house and grounds were acquired by the National Trust.

THE SITE

Drayton Hall is set in the subtropical portion of coastal South Carolina known as the low country. During the Miocene Epoch this region was submerged

(Dunbar 1966:354), and there is ample evidence of this submersion in the excavation of fossilized sharks teeth, clams and bones and petrified wood that are found along with the remains of human activity.

At the time Drayton Hall was built, the low country climate was similar to that of today. There were vast tracts of virgin forest, much of which later was cleared for planting. In certain areas the impoundment of the marshes was undertaken for drainage and farming. Between the 1870s and the 1900s the land along the Ashley River was extensively altered due to the mining of phosphate and its subsequent processing. Strip-mining was carried out on Drayton Hall lands, with most of the mining being done in the area south of the main drive and west of State Highway 61. The south portion was extensively mined with hand tools, the west portion by machine. The extent and nature of these operations shows clearly in a March 1939 aerial photograph of the Ashley River area taken by the Soil Conservation Service of the U.S. Department of Agriculture. The embankments left by both these processes are still clearly visible.

Other industry changed the Drayton Hall landscape as well. During the 20th century, sand was removed from the west side of Route 61, leaving a large burrow pit which is still visible, and selected areas of the property, particularly on the south side of the drive, were commercially logged for hardwood. Loblolly pine was replanted in the cutover areas.

In all, the entire 633 acres that composed the original Drayton holdings have been extensively altered since the time of initial occupation by John Drayton in 1738. Today, with the exception of the lawn adjacent to the house, which has been cleared, most of the property is overgrown with scrub, small trees and vines. Evidence of farming and the extensive drainage system are difficult to discern due to changes in the land and heavy undergrowth. Rice-growing would have been carried on with its accompanying dikes and drainage ditches, and there would have been fields for other crops.

Drayton Hall itself stands on an elevated area surrounded by lower marshes. The adjacent lawn is bounded by a sophisticated system of 18th-century drainage and landscape ditches. A number of the oldest trees in the garden area along the river were lost during the hurricane of 1958, and the area has since become heavily overgrown. Research and photographs indicate that these gardens were laid out on the English park pattern (Drayton, 1802) rather than as formal gardens. Late 19th-century azalea plantings (Japanese hybrids) throughout the garden are still evident, and a marble pedestal for a piece of statuary remains. Other late 18th and early 19th-century landscaping features, such as a small ornamental pond, also remain. A three-tiered mound (c. 1905) in front of the west facade of the house and the fencing that once surrounded the house typify Victorian landscaping.

As previously noted, only one outbuilding from the 18th century remains. However, the diary entries made by Charles Drayton between 1789 and 1817 demonstrate the number and variety of buildings that once played a role in plantation life. Drayton notes repairs or damage to or construction of the following: "Dovecot," 21 July 1789; "potatoe" cellar, 22 October 1789; two offices, 14 September 1791; magazine, 13 August 1794; "loom house," 13 October 1794; poultry house, 24 August 1795; poultry yard fence, 18 March 1796; garden barn, 7 February 1797; "reverbatory furnace for burning shells

to lime," 5 November 1798; brick kiln, 16 November 1797; cotton barn and
cotton stove, 18 November 1797; barracks, 21 July 1802; "Carpenters began to
prepare the timbers for constructing the new range of negroe houses at D.H.,"
18 June 1804; barn, 18-21 August 1804; rice mill and lodge, 10 January 1806;
stables, 20 June 1808; "Began setting the washing kettle in brickwork according
to Rumford," 19 August 1808; wash house, 30 January 1809; mill, 18 March 1812;
tabby corn barn, 7 October 1812; and a pigeon house, 8 January 1817.

ARCHAEOLOGICAL METHOD

The archaeological investigations at Drayton Hall were carried out in three
stages: area survey, test excavations and limited intensive excavations. The
visual area survey was carried out before the commencement of test excavations.
Known sites were located and the areas surrounding the main house were surveyed
for structural and nonstructural remains.

The lawn around Drayton Hall was surveyed (fig. 2) and divided into a 10-foot
square grid system to provide an accurate location of any finds in relation to
known points on the property. Within this grid all excavation units (except
Unit 1) were located. An extensive visual survey and surface collection of
artifacts was made on the lawn and areas immediately surrounding the house.
The excavation of Units 10, 11 and 12 was the result of this intensive surface
collecting. The grid has as its reference base a United States Coast and
Geodetic Survey triangulation monument (Drayton #1, TBM, Elevation 10.96 feet
above sea level at mean low water) on the eastern boundry of the property.
Three test holes were dug around the perimeter of the lawn area to establish
stratigraphic control data.

In areas where architectural features were suspected, the ground was probed
with pointed iron rods in an attempt to locate the exact positions of under-
ground structural remains and thus save fruitless test excavations. Where
probing indicated the presence of structural remains, test units were
excavated, their size depending on the area to be covered. If the test
trenching did indeed yield structural remains or remains of landscaping
features, such as roots, root molds, tree molds and ditches, or otherwise
indicated an area or areas of major importance, such as the flanker buildings,
detailed excavation in units 10 by 10 feet was carried out to define the size
and determine the contents, date, usage and plan of the feature.

Each excavation unit was assigned a provenience control number (unit number)
and strata and features within each unit were assigned a letter as well. All
pertinent data were recorded on provenience cards kept for each unit
(Appendix C). In addition, profile and plan drawings, a survey log,
photographs and a day book were kept as a means of data storage and control.
Before and after completion of the excavation, aerial photographs were taken
of the site (fig. 3).

Detailed excavations at Drayton Hall were carried out in six major areas:
the driveway, the mound, the ground floor of the house, a trash pit, the
south flanker and the area between the south flanker and the south facade
of the main house. Test excavation only was carried out in several other
areas: the area between the house and the river, an area near the large
excavated trash pit, a garbage dump in the woods along the southern boundary
drainage ditch and the 20th-century well. In all, more than 2,100 square
feet of ground were opened for excavation to depths ranging from a few
inches to several feet down to undisturbed subsoil.

The subsoil toward the river consists of a sticky gray clay marl with
occasional nodes of hardened yellow marl (the Younges Formation). In

the immediate area of the house and westward toward the drive, the subsoil changes to a dark yellow brown sandy clay mixed with a tan brown sandy clay. This subsoil contains numerous small, hard nodules of marl with occasional larger ones (Hockley Formation). Farther west the amount of sand overlying the subsoil increases and is a light tan to yellow brown containing almost no marl nodules.

Shovels were used to remove only the sod and topsoil in the excavation areas and also in digging one of the test trenches. Trowels and smaller tools were used to complete the excavations. Quarter-inch mesh screen was used to sift dirt in most of the excavated areas.

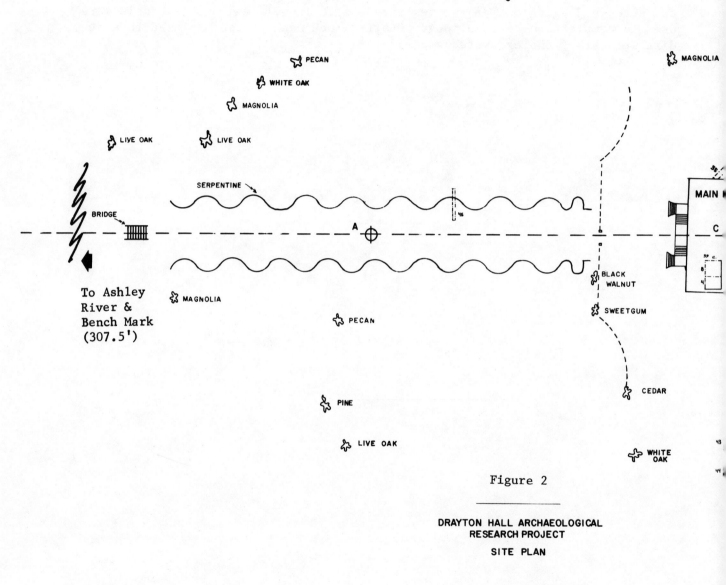

PINE

PECAN

WHITE OAK

MAGNOLIA

MAGNOLIA

LIVE OAK

LIVE OAK

SERPENTINE

MAIN

A

C

BRIDGE

BLACK
WALNUT

To Ashley
River &
Bench Mark
(307.5')

MAGNOLIA

SWEETGUM

PECAN

CEDAR

PINE

LIVE OAK

WHITE
OAK

Figure 2

DRAYTON HALL ARCHAEOLOGICAL
RESEARCH PROJECT

SITE PLAN

—— — —— GRID LINE

— — — — OLD FENCE LINE

— · — · — · EDGE OF EXCAVATION

///// or ▬▬▬ BRICK FOUNDATION

🌳 TREE

(5½ inches = 300 feet)

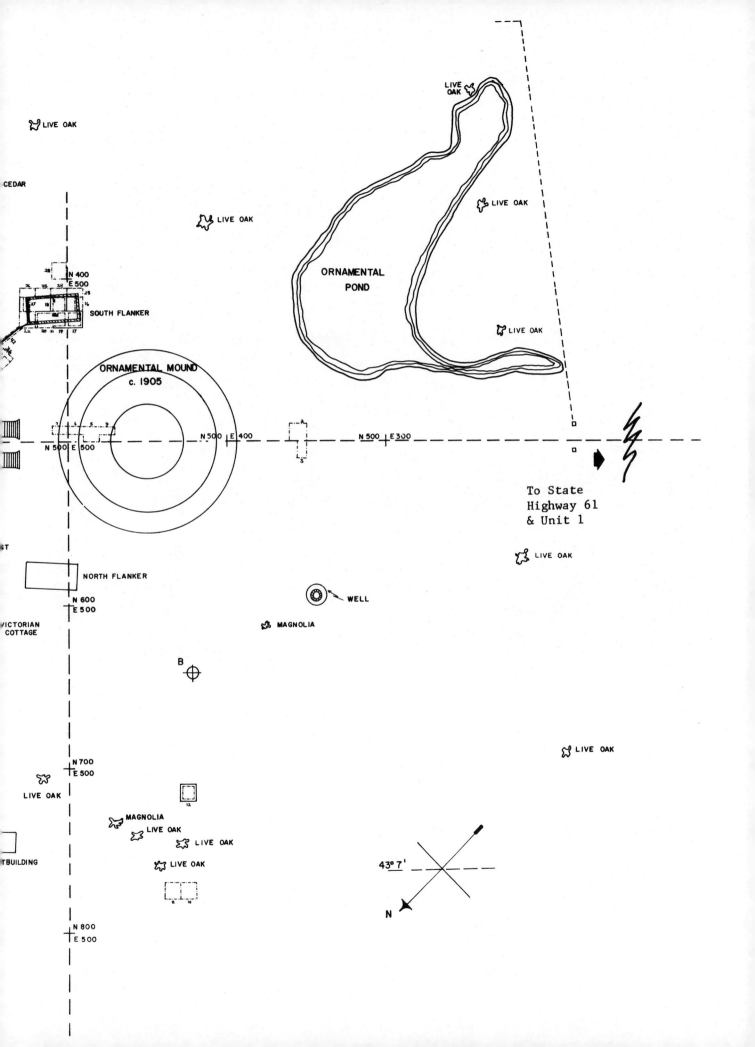

LIVE OAK

CEDAR

LIVE OAK

LIVE
OAK

LIVE OAK

ORNAMENTAL
POND

LIVE OAK

N 400
E 500

SOUTH FLANKER

LIVE OAK

ORNAMENTAL MOUND
c. 1905

N 500 E 400

N 500 E 300

N 500 E 500

To State
Highway 61
& Unit 1

LIVE OAK

NORTH FLANKER

WELL

N 600
E 500

VICTORIAN
COTTAGE

MAGNOLIA

B

LIVE OAK

N 700
E 500

LIVE OAK

MAGNOLIA

LIVE OAK

LIVE OAK

OUTBUILDING

LIVE OAK

43° 7'

N

N 800
E 500

18

Figure 3: Aerial view of west facade Drayton Hall, showing flanker as excavated.

THE EXCAVATIONS

DRIVEWAY AND MOUND EXCAVATIONS

Initial excavations were conducted on the driveway because it was to be regraded and resurfaced in March 1975. At that time the drive was straight and ran one-half mile from State Highway 61 to a set of brick pillars approximately 360 feet from the west facade of the main house. Since the existing drive could not be excavated in its entirety, it was surface collected almost daily during January. The first excavation unit opened (Unit 1) was at the western end of the drive, just inside the entrance pillars on State Highway 61. In this area of comparatively high ground, there were no alterations to the drive; however, evidence of filled ruts and potholes as well as lenticular deposition or lensing of the sandy soil due to rain was discovered. Artifacts consisted largely of brick fragments, window and bottle glass, nails and modern 22 rimfire cartridges. Later, during regrading of the drive, two culverts were laid across the drive. The archaeologists were on hand when the cuttings were made to note and photograph any evidence of changes. Only small scatterings of brick were found.

On-site evidence and the 19th-century photographs indicated that the drive originally crossed the lawn and the area where the present mound is now located, although this portion of the drive evidently fell into disuse some time after the Civil War.

Excavation of the drive as it entered the lawn (Units 2 and 3) revealed that the drainage ditch on the north side of the drive was brick lined and the drive was dirt. The great quantities of brick in the driveway itself were the result of brick debris being used to fill in ruts and potholes. Occupational debris and fireplace and food waste were also discarded in the drive. In the sod and topsoil level (2A) numerous ceramic fragments and glass sherds were recovered along with jasper and chert pebbles, oyster shell, mortar, slate and a fragment of an 18th-century brass furniture pull. Beneath this was a level (2B) that contained a similar variety of artifacts but was excavated separately because of soil color differentiation. The ceramics unearthed ranged from Colono-Indian ware to whitewares, with tin-glazed earthenware and fine lathe-turned basalt wares also present. The variety of debris would indicate that the dirt drive was constantly being filled and graded with trash. A delft tile corner, blue and purple with a carnation motif (fig. 4), dates from the mid-18th century (Noel Hume 1972:291), while a modern lime-green soda bottle fragment was also recovered.

A semicircular intrusion (2C) apparently was a pothole that was filled all at once since it contained only a fragment of a blue transfer-printed willow pattern pearlware plate and an iron padlock (fig. 5). Two linear intrusions (2D and E) were excavated and found to be filled with household debris and brick fragments. These are thought to represent traces of carriage ruts. Below these areas were a series of linear intrusions (2F-I and M) associated with various stages of driveway fill (fig. 6), some containing artifacts and others not. The

20

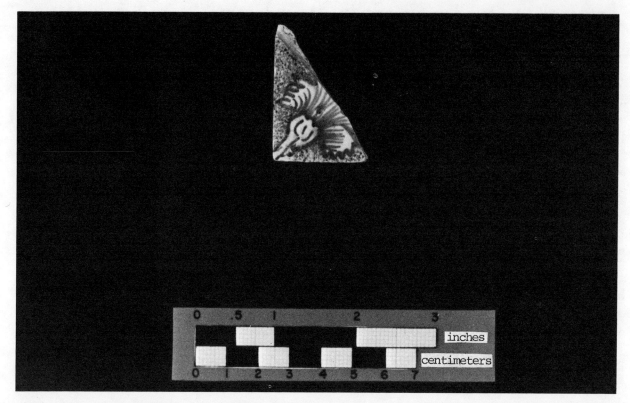

Figure 4: Tin-glazed earthenware tile corner, carnation motif; blue
flower on powder blue background, Unit 2B/BP.

Figure 5: Pearlware, blue transfer-printed plate (willow pattern), and
padlock (2-5/8" at widest point); both Unit 2C.

average thickness of the driveway surface was .96 feet, ranging from a minimum of .72 foot at the southeast end to maximum of 1.29 feet at the center. When Unit 2 was expanded, the sod and topsoil level (2N) again contained great quantities of artifacts, including ceramics, window and bottle glass, nails, bones, shell, brick, roofing tile, slate and tobacco pipe fragments. Beneath the built-up levels of the driveway, a large root mold (2L) was excavated, and the entire unit was taken down to undisturbed subsoil.

Unit 3, north of Unit 2, was opened in an effort to determine the size and makeup of the ditch that lined the north side of the drive. There was no ditch along the south side of the drive, an absence that had been expected since the land slopes away from the drive toward the ornamental pond. The sod and topsoil level (3A) was similar to that found in Unit 2. At the northern-most end of the unit a circular intrusion (3B) was excavated, but it contained only Indian pottery and a brick crumb (fig. 7). There was no post mold, only a round hole. The ditch was excavated along the edge of the drive and was filled with medium to large-sized marl nodules. It contained only fossil remains, which are naturally associated with the marl. Several large root molds were also excavated in this unit and the whole was excavated down to undisturbed subsoil (fig. 6).

Survey of the site and comparison with other plantations of the same period led to the belief that the most likely form for the driveway terminus would be a return, probably circular; however, grass and the lack of clarity in the early photographs hampered a determination of the manner in which the drive ended. In an effort to discover this, a test trench 30 feet long by 5 feet wide was excavated, beginning at the second tier of the mound and moving toward the house in the hope of crossing the drive. The evidence indicated that a return was located approximately 50 feet from the steps of the west portico and that it now underlies the second tier of the mound (fig. 8).

Unit 5 was expanded 5 feet to the north to confirm the location of the drive return. This portion of the drive contained considerably less fill than found in the lower portion. As the excavations proceeded toward the house, the sod and topsoil levels of Units 6 and 7 were found to contain a variety of arti-facts, including ceramics, metal, bottle and window glass, nails and stone. A level of dark brown sandy loam (6B) was then excavated. Aside from the usual quantities of household debris, this area contained large pockets of finely crushed gravel, which also appeared in level 7B. It is thought that this may represent a graveled court that spanned the distance between the driveway return and the stairs (fig. 9). This theory was later given con-firmation by written evidence: On 31 March 1790, Charles Drayton wrote in his diary, "Began yesterday to smooth the surface of the court yard."

No artifacts were found in a modern posthole and mold that were excavated in Unit 6 (6C and D). Subsequently, a photograph of the west facade of the house and the area in front of it was acquired from the Drayton family. This photo-graph, dating from the period 1875-1900, shows a circular rose garden fenced by a square-post and rail fence, with smaller square posts inside the fence. It is reasonably certain that the posthole in Unit 7 and one in Unit 9 were both part of the rose garden fence. In Unit 6 the old topsoil (6E) was removed down to undisturbed subsoil; it contained very few artifacts, largely glass, ceramics, nails and brick fragments. Unit 7 was excavated only to the surface of the old topsoil, and there was a circular posthole

Figure 6

Units 3 & 2
East Profile

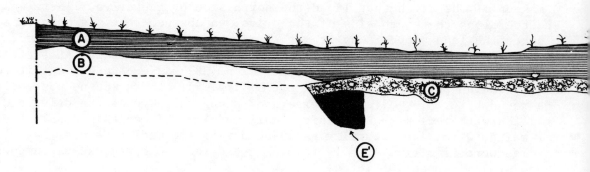

Units 2 & 3
West Profile

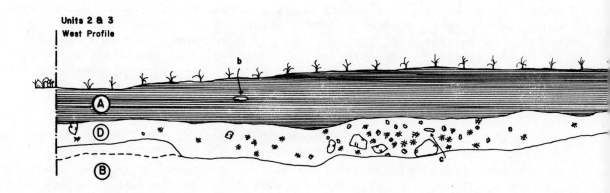

A   Dark brown sandy loam with numerous brick fragments   (Topsoil)

B   Mottled tan-brown and yellow-brown sandy-clayey loam   (Subsoil)

C   Very dark brown sandy loam mottled with 50% tan-yellow clayey loam   (Driveway ditch)

D   Very dark brown sandy loam mottled with 10% tan-yellow clayey loam & heavy concentration of brick fragments and mortar flecks   (Driveway fill)

E   Very dark brown sandy loam with occasional brick crumbs (Root mold)

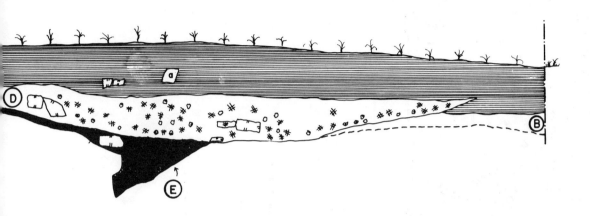

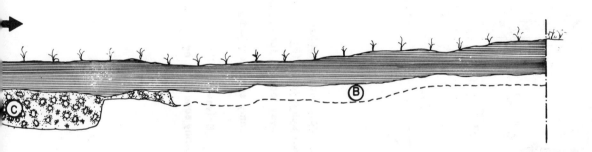

E'   Tan - brown sandy loam mottled with 20% yellow sand & gray- brown
       loamy sand (Root mold)

a & c – Ceramic fragment
b   – Padlock
✳   – Mortar
▭   – Brick
❧   – Marl

0   .5   1   2   3
                                feet

24

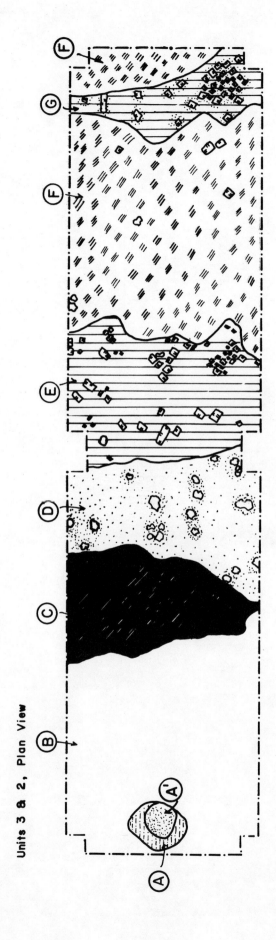

Units 3 & 2, Plan View

N

Figure 7

A   Dark brown sandy loam (Post hole)

A' Very dark brown sandy loam (Post mold)

B   Light tan-brown loamy sand mottled with 40% tan-yellow clayey loam (Subsoil)

C   Tan-yellow clayey loam mottled with 20% dark gray-brown sandy loam (Root mold)

D   Very dark brown sandy loam mottled with 50% tan-yellow clayey loam & tan-brown loamy sand
    with numerous marl nodules (Driveway ditch)

E   Very dark brown sandy loam mottled with 20% tan-brown loamy sand & a heavy concentration
    of brick bats and crumbs (Driveway rut)

F   Dark gray-brown sandy loam with occasional brick crumbs (Driveway fill)

G   Dark brown sandy loam mottled with 20% tan-brown loamy sand & a heavy concentration
    of brick bats and crumbs (Driveway rut)

0 .5 1   2   3
              feet

(7E) which had been packed with brick for filling but contained no datable artifacts. There is no explanation for the posthole, although it is possible that the fencing around the roses underwent alterations.

Since a segment of the mound was excavated to find the driveway terminus, it was decided to complete exploration of this landscape feature and determine the original ground level. Unit 9 was opened into the third (top) tier of the mound. The mound fill itself consists largely of tightly compacted clay and marl, both major components of the subsoil (fig. 8). The fill contained little human debris but did contain numerous sharks' teeth and fossil clams. There is speculation that the fill may have been obtained from the dredging of the ornamental pond, which the Drayton family states took place during the early 20th century. Nothing was located to contradict the 1905 date given for the mound construction.

It should be noted that the excavations of the lawn portions of the property in the vicinity of the house indicated that extensive regrading took place some time in the recent past. A fill ranging from 4 to 8 inches in depth was discovered over the driveway, the mound and the flanker; this may have been deposited during the mound construction, since landscaping was obviously taking place at that time.

GROUND FLOOR EXCAVATIONS

Concurrent with the driveway and mound excavations, investigation of the northeast ground floor room within Drayton Hall was undertaken (Units 4 and 8). This particular room was selected because it is the only one of the five ground floor rooms (fig. 10) with a dirt floor. The other floors are of brick, paving tile or stone. The quantities of brick dust and occasional whole brick indicate that the floor of the northeast room was also paved at one time. A plaster ceiling in the room either collapsed or was removed some time after removal of the brick. The presence of this plaster ceiling is confirmed by lath and plaster scars on the exposed beams in this and all the other ground floor rooms. The plaster ceilings have been replaced by circular-sawn board ceilings.

Information on the use of the northeast room is sketchy due to heavy under-mining of the floor by rodents and to trenches dug along the walls in the 1950s to aid in termite extermination. The recovered artifacts and the rodent burrows themselves, however, would indicate that the room was used for food storage. Among the remains recovered were hickory nut shells, pig and sheep bones, rodent jaws and long bones, bird bones, oyster shell, fish scales and bones, egg shell fragments and corn cobs. Although preservation of organic materials would be enhanced by their being indoors, this location does not entirely account for the presence of so much material, because the ground floor is extremely damp much of the time. After Unit 4 was left unattended for several months, two fiddler crabs and a frog skeleton were discovered in the unit, indicating its high moisture content. The occurrence of so much organic material under these conditions indicates possible food storage. A large fireplace crane that fits into the fireplace in the central room indi-cates that some food preparation took place on the ground floor. It would be logical to have food storage nearby.

Figure 8

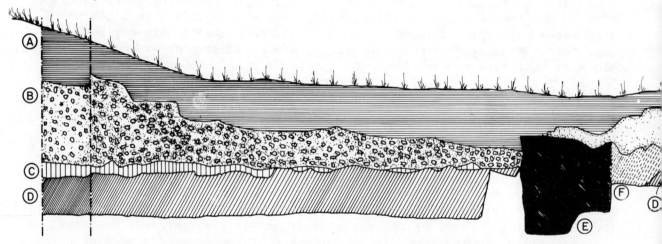

Units 9 & 5, North Profile

A Dark brown sandy loam (Topsoil)

B Dark brown sandy loam mottled with 50% marl nodules & occasional brick flecks (Mound fill)

C Very dark brown clayey loam mottled with 50% light gray clay & occasional brick and mortar flecks (Mound fill)

D Dark brown sandy loam (Old topsoil)

E Very dark gray-brown sandy loam mottled with 10% tan-gray clayey loam (Flower bed?)

F Dark brown clayey loam

G Dark brown clayey loam mottled with 50% tan-brown clay & occasional marl nodules

H Light tan-brown clayey loam mottled with 5% marl nodules (Subsoil)

I Very dark brown clayey loam with occasional brick & mortar flecks

J Very dark brown sandy loam

K Light gray clay

L Very dark gray-brown clayey loam mottled with 10% light gray clay (Mound fill)

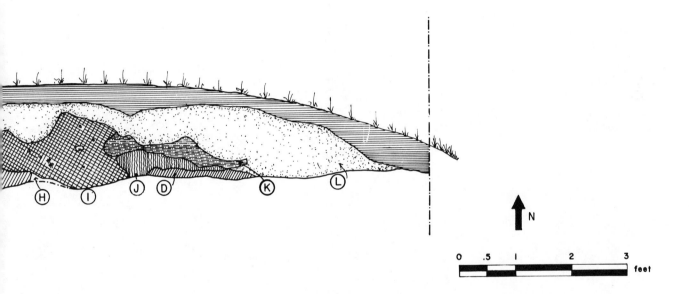

H   I   J   D   K   L

N

0   .5   1   2   3
feet

llh & cec
6 – 16 – 76

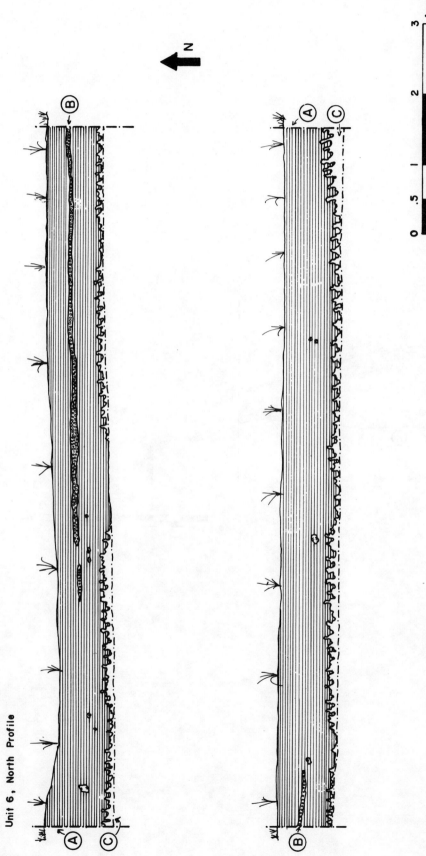

Unit 6, North Profile

N

A   Dark brown sandy loam with occasional brick flecks (Topsoil & Old topsoil)

B   Dark brown sandy loam with a heavy concentration of gravel   (Courtyard fill)

C   Tan - yellow & tan - brown sandy loam (Subsoil)

llh
6-16-76

Figure 9

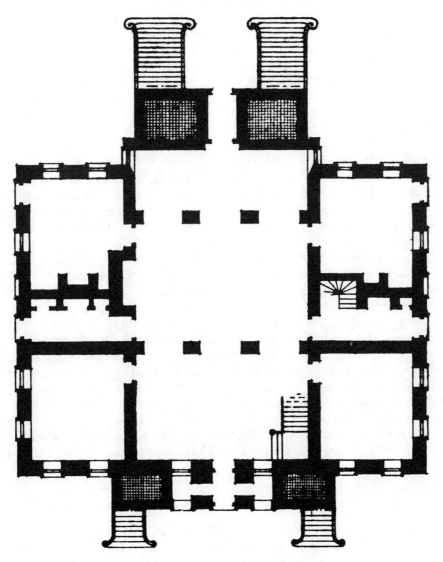

Figure 10: Ground floor plan. (Measured by Albert
Simons; drawn by Frank E. Seel and Lewis B. Middleton)

In conjunction with the work of the historical architect, two areas of the floor in the main room were excavated (Units 39 and 40). Unit 39 was in front of the northeast room doorway and Unit 40 in front of the southwest room doorway. It was hypothesized that the paving-stone floor currently in evidence was not original, and this was confirmed in the excavations. Directly beneath the stone flooring (of blocks 1.5 by 1.5 by 2 feet) were deposits of mortar that were concentrated in the cracks (due to frost and settling) and in the joints between the stones, indicating that the floor was grouted some time after its original installation. The stones must have received rough cut because there are numerous chips beneath the stones that cannot be accounted for by simple cracking. Underlying the mortar was a layer of coarse crushed oyster shell, apparently used to level the floor before the stones were laid. Beneath the oyster shell was a thin layer of reddish brick dust. In lifting stones in other areas of the floor, traces of brick dust and bricks were also found. These bricks were badly deteriorated and it appeared that most of them had been removed from the floor while others were left in place because they had deteriorated.

Brick and mortar deterioration has always been of concern on the ground floor. In places where the mortar is exposed it is crumbling out of the joints, and most of the brick walls have been plastered over several times in an attempt to halt this deterioration. The brick floor in the southeast room also suffers from moisture seepage and salts are efflorescing onto the brick floor.

Aside from the question of whether or not the floor was brick (although it appears likely that it was), the stones were certainly laid some time after 1800. This date is substantiated by artifactual evidence. Although some delft and porcelain were recovered, a small fragment of a whiteware plate provided a terminus post quem of c. 1820 for the exposed floor. It was not possible to determine how long the floor was exposed before bricking or whether it was exposed between the bricking and the stone paving. Again, there were rodent burrows throughout the area. An undisturbed segment of the interior builder's trench was discovered in Unit 40 in front of the large brick pier. (The builder's trench was also located in Unit 4 (fig. 11). Only a small portion of it remained beneath the termite trench, and it contained only a few crumbled bricks. The builder's trench on the interior was noticeably wider than it was on the exterior, indicating that the bricklayers worked from the outside.

INVESTIGATION OF A TRASH DEPOSIT

The next area to be excavated was along the north border of the lawn. Excavation was undertaken there when a surface survey revealed a heavy concentration of occupational and architectural debris in quantities sufficient to indicate the possibility of a structure at that location. Extremely large quantities of loosely compacted debris were removed, but no structural remains were discovered. An additional unit (11) was opened to the east of the initial one (Unit 10) in the hope of finding a structure (fig. 12), but this unit also failed to yield any structural remains. The great quantities of building materials removed from these two units indicate that a building either collapsed or was razed in the area. A total of 0.6 cubic foot (18.5 quarts) of slate, 9.9 cubic feet (299 quarts) of brick and 60 roofing tile fragments (unglazed buff paste earthenware) were recovered, along with more than 1,200 nails and 90 pieces of architectural stone (e.g., paving

Unit 4, North Profile

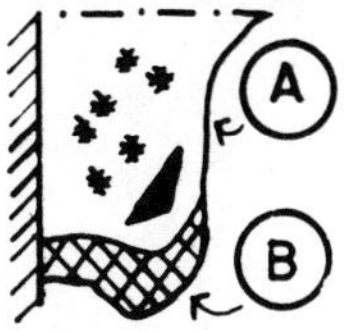

A   Very dark brown sandy loam with plaster &
     mortar fragments (Termite trench)

B   Dark brown sandy loam   (Interior construction ditch)

    Plaster fragment

feet

N ⬆

Figure 11

Unit 10, North Profile

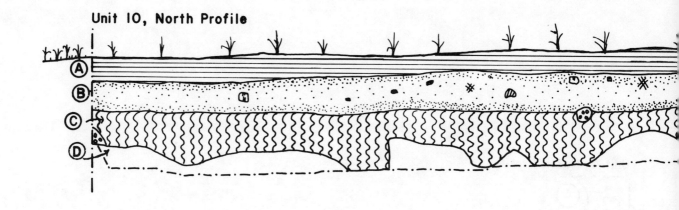

Unit 11, North Profile

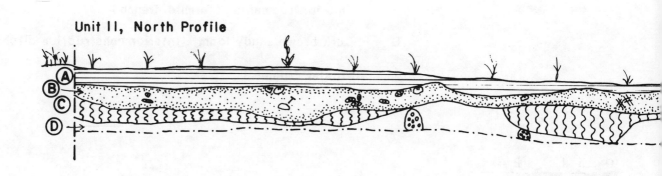

Unit 11, East Profile

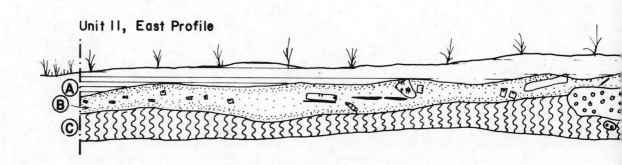

A Very dark gray-brown sandy loam (Topsoil)

B Very dark gray-brown sandy loam with numerous brick fragments (Rubble

C Dark gray-brown sandy loam mottled with 30% marl nodules (Old top

D Tan-gray sandy loam with numerous marl nodules (Subsoil)

◻ Roofing tile

▨ Brick   ⟩ Nail

— Slate   #⃰# Mortar

🦪 Oyster shell

◉ Root

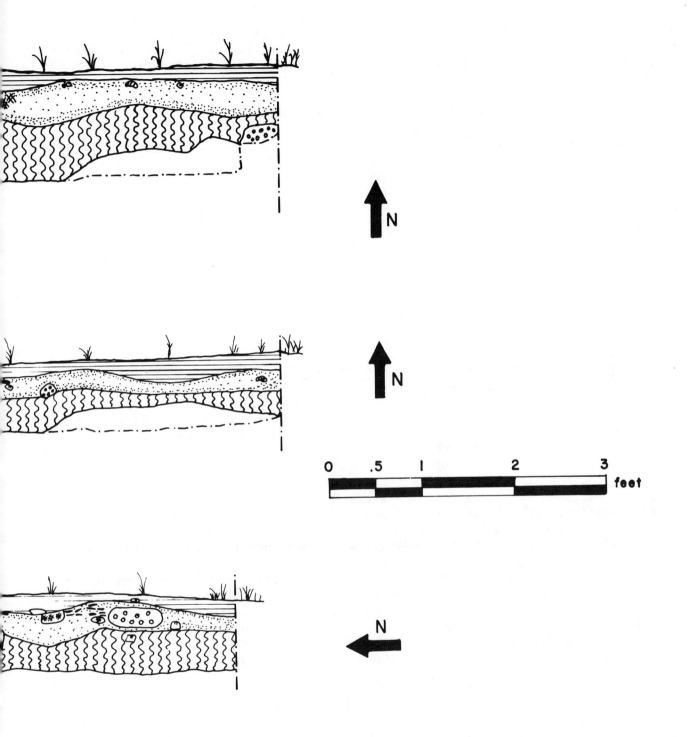

Figure 12

stone). More than 7,500 artifacts were recovered from these two areas alone. It subsequently was learned that this debris originally was located approximately 45 feet to the south and was bulldozed to its present location about 10 years ago.

The trash was deposited near the small brick office (fig. 2) and is associated with a presently unlocated structure. It may be one of the two offices referred to in Drayton's diary entry of 14 September 1791, or it is possible that the debris represents a building removed to construct the office. The recovery of an Irish George II (young-head) halfpence (fig. 13), which would have been minted between 1736 and 1755 (Noel Hume 1973:166) was one of the earliest finds in the deposit, while the presence of several sherds of whiteware indicates that the debris was accumulating at least until c. 1820. The mixed, unstratified nature of this material makes it very difficult to draw any conclusions about it. Analysis of the recovered material shows, in general, a concentration of artifacts from the period 1775 to 1800, which is confirmed by a calculated mean ceramic date of 1790.3 (Appendix D, table 1).*

SOUTH FLANKER EXCAVATIONS

In May 1975 intensive archaeological investigation of the south flanker foundation was undertaken (Units 16-27). The entire foundation was exposed to varying depths. It was found that the walls consist of five complete courses of brick with remnants of a sixth course visible in some areas. Only the mortar in the highest remaining course was pointed; the mortar was made from burned oyster shells, which are rich in lime content. (Charles Drayton constructed a reverbatory furnace for the burning of shells on the property and he recorded in his diary [14 September 1791] the output and shell type used. While Drayton provided dimensions for the furnace, he failed to give its location, although it would be reasonable to assume that it was near the river since the shell arrived by boat.) From the pattern of destruction, it is obvious that the flanker foundation was plowed under (figs. 14 and 15).

Photographs from the late 19th century show that the flankers were two-story brick structures with central chimneys. The first floor in each was raised above ground level and was entered from an outside staircase of three-tiered brick construction. From excavation it was determined that the south flanker fireplace opened only on one side (east) and that there were two rooms on the first floor. The foundations for the entry stairway were uncovered along the north foundation wall in Units 19 and 20.

Excavations were carried out in detail along the northern half of the south flanker, which measures 17 by 33 feet, with the long dimension running east-west. The sod and topsoil levels in Units 16-27 contained very few artifacts, with the exception of the area that would have been directly under the entry

----

*Mean ceramic dates for structural and nonstructural features were determined by using South's Mean Ceramic Dating Formula, an explanation of which appears in Appendix D along with the mean ceramic dates established for some of the ceramics recovered at Drayton Hall. Appendix E explains the dating formula used for pipe stems and also provides the dates resulting from use of that formula.

Figure 13: Irish halfpennies, obverse and reverse. Left,
George II young-head, Unit 11C/BEC; center, George III
young-head, Unit 38B IVa; right, George II young-head,
Unit 17L/CI. (All actual size)

Figure 14

UNITS 17, 18, 19, 20, 21 & 22 - PLAN VIEW

A   Very dark brown sandy loam mottled with 20% tan-brown clayey loam (Old top soil)

B   Very dark brown sandy loam mottled with 30% dark gray-brown clayey loam & 20% oyster shell (Trash pit)

C   Very dark brown sandy loam mottled with 30% tan-brown clayey loam, 10% tan-yellow clayey loam & 30% brick and mortar rubble (Interior construction ditch)

D   Very dark brown sandy loam mottled with 20% tan-brown clayey loam with occasional brick and mortar flecks (Interior construction debris)

D'   Bright red-brown sandy clay loam with occasional brick bats (Interior construction debris, chimney)

E   Dark brown sandy loam mottled with 30% yellow-brown clayey loam & 10% mortar and brick flecks (Post hole)

E'   Dark brown sandy loam mottled with 10% tan-brown sandy loam (Post hole)

F   Medium dark brown sandy loam mottled with 20% mortar & 40% brick dust, with occasional brick bats and whole brick (Exterior occupation debris)

F'   Tan-brown clay mottled with 10% dark gray-brown & occasional charcoal and brick flecks (Exterior occupation debris)

G   Very dark brown sandy loam mottled with 20% mortar flecks & occasional brick bats (Exterior construction ditch)

H   Dark brown sandy loam mottled with 10% tan-brown clayey loam occasional brick flecks (Interior occupation debris)

I   Dark brown sandy loam with numerous brick bats (Interior destruction

J   Loosely compacted mortar mixed with brick dust (Chimney destruction

K   Tan-brown loamy sand (Chimney construction?)

L   Dark brown sandy loam mottled with 10% tan-brown clayey loam, numerous brick bats and crumbs & large mortar fragments and crumbs (Interior destruction debris)

M   Chimney foundation

N   Exterior entrance stairway foundation

O   Very dark gray-brown sandy loam with numerous brick bats (Exterior destruction debris)

P   Very dark brown sandy loam (Root mold)

R   Unexcavated

S   Very dark brown sandy loam mottled with 20% tan-yellow clayey loam & 50% brick bats (Root mold)

llh
6-11-76

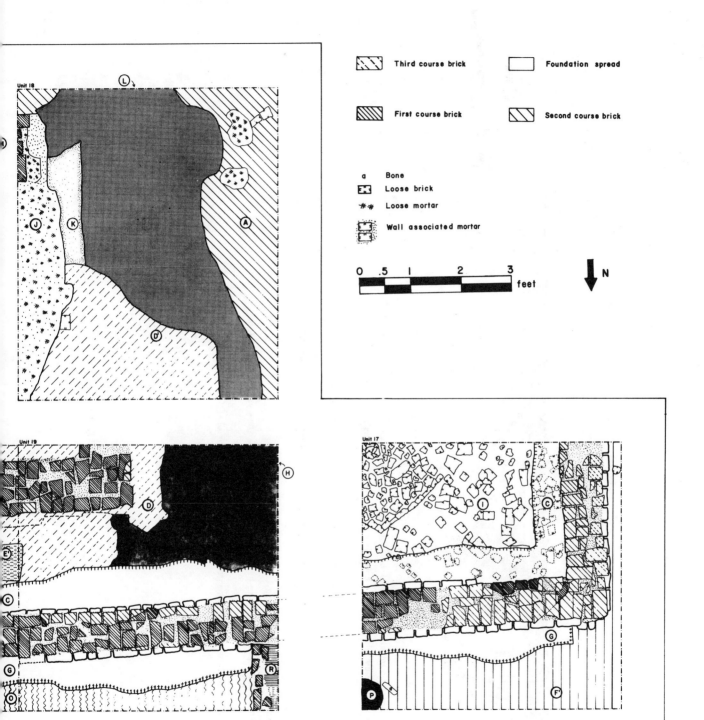

Third course brick

Foundation spread

First course brick

Second course brick

a   Bone
   Loose brick
   Loose mortar
   Wall associated mortar

0 .5 1   2   3

feet

N

Unit 18

Unit 19

Unit 17

38

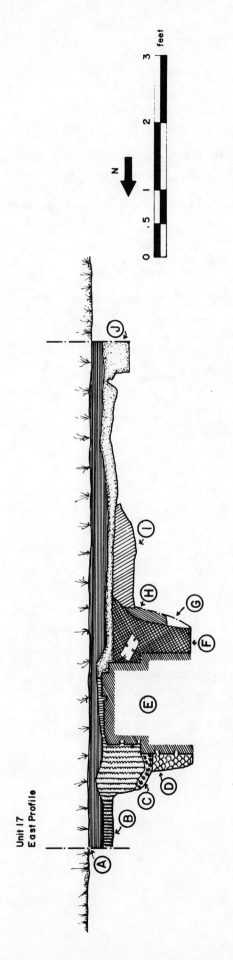

Unit 17
East Profile

A   Very dark gray - brown sandy loam with occasional brick crumbs   (Topsoil)

B   Very dark gray - brown sandy loam with numerous brick fragments (Exterior destruction debris)

C   Mortar

D   Very dark brown sandy loam mottled with 20% mortar flecks   (Exterior construction ditch)

E   Flanker foundation

F   Very dark brown sandy loam mottled with 30% yellow - brown sandy loam   (Interior construction ditch)

G   Tan - brown clayey loam   (Subsoil)

H   Very dark gray - brown sandy loam   (Old topsoil)

I   Dark brown sandy loam mottled with 40% tan - brown clayey loam & 20% tan - yellow clayey loam   (Interior construction debris)

J   Dark brown sandy loam with numerous brick fragments   (Interior destruction debris)

▨   Brick

Figure 15

N

0   .5   1   2   3
feet

llh & cec
6-14-76

stairway. Since the stairs had been removed as early as the 1870s, a fact known from the photographic record, material would tend to accumulate more rapidly in the area of the doorway. Typical of the entire lawn area, the variety of artifacts in the sod and topsoil around the flanker ranges from nails (both old and new), tobacco pipe fragments, whiteware and prehistoric Indian ware to modern bottle glass fragments--i.e., unassociable mixed fill.

A level of destruction debris was located immediately below the sod and top-soil. When this level was exposed, there was a clear distinction between the soils on the exterior and the interior of the foundation. All interior and exterior areas therefore were excavated separately and an interesting distinction between the contents of these two areas was perceived. The concentrations of brick rubble were much higher on the interior, whereas the nail concentrations were far greater on the exterior. This led to the hypothesis that the interior was cleaned out first and then the building was razed. This is further confirmed by the fact that the concentrations of artifacts other than building materials are all high on the exterior and very sparse on the interior.

The thickness of the destruction debris on the exterior, (Units 17B, 19B, 20B, 20C, 21B, 22B) varied from a minimum of 0.04 foot to a maximum of 0.79 foot with the average thickness being 0.38 foot. On the interior of the building (Units 17C, 18B, 18C, 19C, 20D, 21C, 22C), the thickness of the destruction level ranged from 0.07 to 0.74 foot with an average of 0.27 foot. The arti-fact concentration was heaviest outside the stairway foundation and lightest within (fig. 16).

It is of great interest to note that the placement of the doorway would have been difficult to determine on the basis of the artifact distribution alone. From the analysis of, and comparison between, the destruction rubble on the interior and exterior, the general method of destruction can be hypothesized. It is most likely that the building was first completely emptied and then the interior razed, including dismembering of the flooring and the framing. As noted in table 1, the material on the interior consisted of three times more brick and four times more pieces of architectural stone than that on the exterior. Conversely, the number of nails on the exterior was more than six times greater than on the interior and the number of household items such as glass, ceramics, buttons, beads, pipes, etc., was consistently greater. On the exterior there were, in fact, more than eight times the number of arti-facts found than on the interior, a discovery that raises the question of what was occurring outside the doorway, since there were very few artifacts. there. From the floor plan, it can be seen that the passageway between the entryway and the chimney was very narrow. Assuming that the flooring and framing of the building were being removed (as the vast quantities of nails would indicate), it would not have been possible or desirable to turn the corner to take the materials out the door. Therefore, it is most likely that the windows were used for this purpose and would have been far more convenient. This assumption is based on an analysis of the distribution of recovered artifacts similar to that put forward by South (1977) with reference to the swing of doors, namely that one can determine which way a door swung by analysis of the varying amounts of material around it. Without knowing what the south flanker looked like, it would be possible to determine the number and approximate location of the windows. In this case, the information on the door would be misleading without the presence of the stairway foundations

40

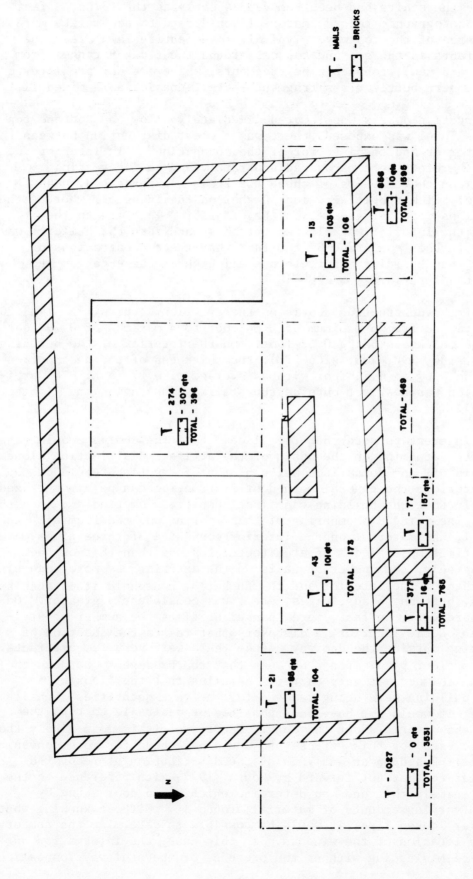

DESTRUCTION DEBRIS - INTERIOR vs. EXTERIOR

Figure 16

TABLE 1

ARTIFACT CONCENTRATIONS: INTERIOR AND EXTERIOR DESTRUCTION DEBRIS

| | EXTERIOR | | | | | | | INTERIOR | | | | | | | |
	17B	19B	20B	20C	21B	22B	TOTAL	17C	18B	18C	19C	20D	21C	22C	TOTAL
Brick cu. ft.	0.3	3.5	0.5	1.6	0.1	0	6	3.4	3.9	6.3	1.2	2	0.1	2.8	19.7
Nails	856	0	377	64	13	1,027	2,337	13	150	124	40	0	3	21	351
Ceramics	110	24	89	17	6	626	872	23	97	61	9	16	8	35	249
Window glass	98	10	126	23	0	226	483	1	32	4	10	1	1	2	51
Bottle glass	161	34	77	32	13	709	1,026	8	57	19	12	5	2	1	104
Tobacco pipes	27	5	3	4	1	50	90	5	13	7	2	3	0	7	37
Table glass	86	32	11	1	1	11	142	3	17	2	2	0	2	2	28
Buttons	18	0	0	1	0	8	27	0	0	3	0	0	0	1	4
Beads	5	1	0	0	0	2	8	2	1	0	0	0	0	0	3
Furniture metal	2	0	1	0	0	10	13	0	2	0	0	0	0	0	2
Lead ammunition	4	0	2	1	0	3	10	0	1	0	0	0	0	0	1
Mammal bones	135	0	53	145	14	173	520	27	156	70	19	11	6	26	315
Architectural stone	4	0	2	2	1	0	9	6	6	21	1	0	0	0	34
Total	1,595	106	765	312	51	3,531	6,360	106	55	341	105	46	22	104	779

and one might be led to hypothesize that the stairs had still been in place. However, barring such factors, it seems this is an important use of archaeological data, indicating not only window location, but also the probable method of destruction of the building and its description.

Two discernible levels of destruction were removed from Unit 18, located entirely within the flanker foundations and containing the partial remains of the south leg of the chimney foundation. The first level was part of the general building destruction, but the lower one was associated with the robbing out of the back (west) side of the chimney foundation. This portion of the chimney foundation, with the exception of a small portion in Unit 19, was destroyed, probably to reuse the bricks. Immediately below the destruction debris was a level of brick-red brown sandy loam with occasional brickbats, evidently traces of the chimney construction, underlain by old topsoil.

The next area of excavation was a very thin level of occupational debris, which was found in Units 17, 19, 20, 21 and 22. The thickness of this level ranged from 0.01 to 0.54 foot with an average thickness of 0.19 foot. No traces of an occupation level were discernible in Unit 18, which presumably was destroyed when the chimney foundation was razed. In Units 16 and 23-27, excavations were not carried beneath the destruction level. In Unit 17, both an interior and an exterior occupation level were excavated; in Unit 19 only an interior occupation level was discovered, a finding readily explained by the fact that the brick stairway would have covered this entire area. In Unit 20, only an exterior occupation level in the eastern portion outside the stair foundation was found (the interior was not excavated); in Unit 21 only a small interior occupation level was excavated (exterior not opened), but in Unit 22 both interior and exterior occupation levels were excavated. This "leap-frog" method was employed because intensive test excavations rather than complete excavations were desired. Because the site is to be stabilized, that is, neither destroyed nor reconstructed, it was reasonable to leave large portions unexcavated for future detailed digging. Balks over certain critical areas were also left in place for this reason.

Only a small amount of occupational debris (16 artifacts) was found on the interior of the foundation, while on the exterior a great quantity of household debris was recovered (fig. 17). This leads to the conclusion that the air space between the ground and the first floor was not used at all, and also that the flooring above (probably wood on joists) was well sealed. It does not seem reasonable to assume a lack of building usage, since the quantity of artifacts on the exterior, in both the destruction and occupation levels, points to heavy use of the flanker. It is possible that the flooring was installed with splines as it is in the main house, which would prevent the pulling apart of floorboards and thus limit the deposition of artifacts on the ground below.

Outside the east wall of the flanker foundation a large trash deposit was discovered and excavated (Unit 22N). This pit itself appears to have resulted from the removal of a tree and is deep and irregular, cutting below the construction ditch along this wall. The pit is bounded on the northeast by a two-course-high, one-course-wide brick wall leading toward the main house. It is hypothesized that there was a door on the east (back) wall of the flanker, a theory generated by two observations. The first is the placement of the trash pit and the knowledge that household garbage was commonly thrown out the nearest convenient door (South 1977). However, this alone would not be sufficient evidence of a door, since a window could have been used for the same purpose. A second factor was the connection between the main house and the flanker, a continuous wall with

43

OCCUPATION DEBRIS – INTERIOR vs. EXTERIOR

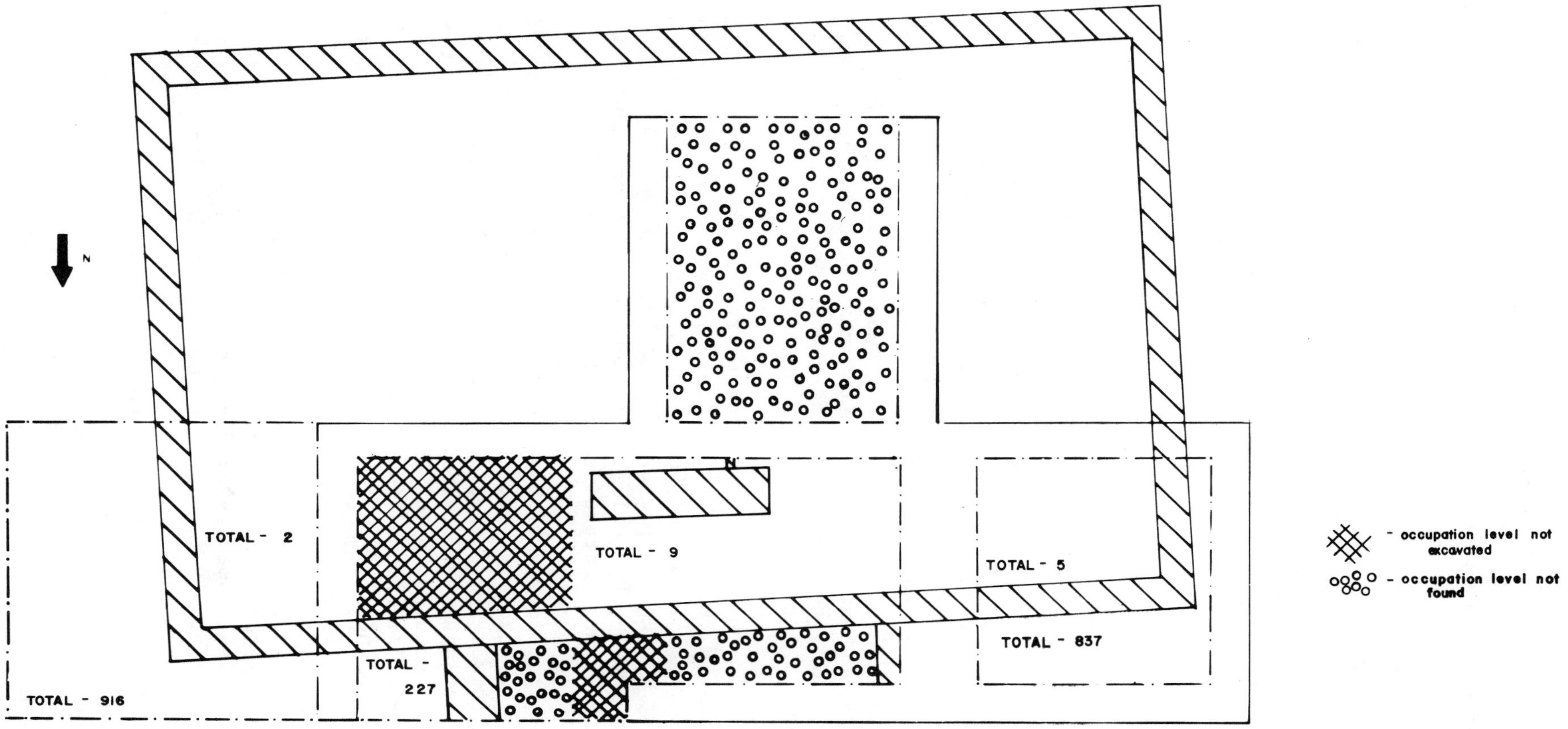

Figure 17

- occupation level not excavated

- occupation level not found

TOTAL - 5

TOTAL - 837

TOTAL - 9

TOTAL - 227

TOTAL - 2

TOTAL - 916

no gate. It seems unlikely that servants would have scaled the wall or gone into the front door of the main house from the front door of the flanker. Therefore, a door from the east wall with a path leading to the central side door of the house would be a reasonable assumption, especially with the evidence provided by the trash pit. But confirmation of this hypothesis will have to await further investigation.

A level of tan brown clay mottled with 10 percent dark gray brown sandy loam and occasional charcoal and brick flecks was discovered immediately below the main occupation level in Unit 17. In no other area was this unique feature found. This level (17J) also contained a number of artifacts, including a diamond-cut glass rhinestone. It is suspected that this level of clay represents a leveling of the area immediately in front of the flanker. The ground slopes noticeably from a low point along the western portion of the building to a high along the eastern end, and the builders may have found a level yard desirable.

Beneath the occupation level, a level of construction debris was found in all units, along with several construction features and the builder's trench. The exterior trench in Units 17, 19, 20, 21 and 22 was excavated plus the interior one in Units 17 and 19. In all cases, the builder's trench on the exterior was considerably narrower than that on the interior, indicating that the bricks were laid from the outside. There was no builder's trench visible for the chimney foundation. The trench on the exterior ranged from a maximum depth of 1.05 feet to a minimum of 0.57 foot and always extended as far as but not beyond the bottom of the initial course of brick. Artifacts found in the exterior trench did not prove particularly helpful in dating the house construction, with the exception of one sherd of creamware found in Unit 17H.

On the interior, the builder's trench depth ranged from 0.43 foot to 1.34 feet. In this trench, as on the exterior, there were sherds of Colono-Indian ware and dark green bottle glass; the most common ceramic type was tin-glazed earthenware, and there were a few pieces of porcelain, as well as tobacco pipe fragments and animal bone. The builder's trench in all cases went down into the subsoil and had no other features underlying it.

In addition to the builder's trench, there were areas of construction debris underlying the occupation or destruction debris, containing very few artifacts. The artifacts that were recovered were similar to those found in the builder's trench (e.g., porcelain, Colono-Indian ware, tin-glazed earthenware, rhenish stoneware, coarse earthenware and one creamware sherd). In addition, a second George II (young-head) Irish halfpence was discovered in Unit 17L. This was minted between 1736 and 1755 and provides a definite terminus post quem for the building.

The presence of two creamware sherds in the construction areas raises interesting questions regarding the construction date. The two sherds are of the deeper yellow that Noel Hume (1972:125-6) brackets as being manufactured between 1762 and 1780. However, it is possible that these two pieces represent contamination of the level, either by rodent or root action. Alternatively, it may be that these particular sherds represent an extremely early arrival of creamware in the colonies or it may be that the flanker was not constructed until c. 1765. This question may only be resolved through further excavation. It is safe to state, however, that the flankers were certainly constructed no earlier than the main house and probably within 20-25 years of its construction.

In addition to the builder's trench and the construction levels, several other features can be associated with the period of construction. A one-foot-deep posthole was excavated in Unit 17 but yielded no artifacts. The post may have served as a supporting pier for the floor above.

In Unit 22 a square intrusion was excavated in the interior northeast corner of the foundation, revealing a posthole and post mold. Both overlay the builder's trench and perhaps represent a scaffolding hole and post. Neither component yielded any datable artifacts. A second square intrusion, a definite scaffolding hole, was excavated in Unit 21 outside the north chimney foundation leg, inside the foundation of the flanker. This hole and mold intruded into the subsoil and lay between the builder's trench and the chimney. The artifacts from this hole are very similar to those found in the builder's trench.

Another posthole, half of which intruded into the builder's trench, was excavated in Unit 19. This posthole evidently dates from much later than the period of construction, since it contained fragments of whiteware and intruded into the ditch. It is under the area of the stairway, would also postdate its destruction and is perhaps associated with the period of destruction.

It is interesting to note the quantities of Colono-Indian ceramics found in the construction areas. In the trench there were eight pieces of ceramic of Indian manufacture, as against a total of 27 sherds of other types. South (1974) notes the presence of slaves or poor white laborers during the construction of Fort Moultrie, on Sullivan's Island, S.C., a few miles from Charleston, which might account for the Colono-Indian ware found there. It is probable that slaves were used in the construction of Drayton Hall, too, as John Drayton is known to have had large slave holdings. The Colono-Indian ware might then be attributed to the slaves.

In Unit 19 one large feature was discovered for which no firm explanation has been found, but it may be a large tree root mold of a tree that was removed before construction of the flanker. The hole is about 4 feet deep and appears on both sides of the foundation wall. There is no break in the wall at this point, and the hole is apparently not a cellar. It appears to have been filled before construction and contained only a few artifacts (e.g., brick, bone and a few ceramics). The hole terminates before it reaches the chimney foundation.

It is hypothesized that the south flanker at one time served as a supplementary kitchen, and possibly also as the bake house. The evidence of a large fireplace in the flanker, along with the absence of any bake ovens in the main house kitchen and the lack of mention of any separate building for baking in the documents leads to the belief that at least a portion of the south flanker was used for this purpose.

It is interesting to note that the mean ceramic dates for the exterior destruction rubble, 1790.4 (Appendix D, table 2) and for the interior rubble, 1786.7 (Appendix D, table 3) vary only slightly from that calculated for the occupation level, 1788.5 (Appendix D, table 4). This latter date is only two years earlier than the exterior rubble and is actually two years later than the interior destruction debris. Destruction debris is expected to contain the material that may have remained in a building, been deposited during its demolition, accumulated after its destruction or all three, in contrast to occupational debris, which is material deposited during the course of a building's useful life span.

It is known that the south flanker stood until at least 1893 and possibly into the 20th century (but not later than the 1930s). From this it might be expected that the building would show a median occupation date of approximately 1832 (based on conservative dates of 1765 for construction and 1900 for destruction). That the dates, both occupation and destruction, cluster around the period 1785-1790 is of great interest. Looking at these dates, which are mean and not absolute dates, one gets the impression that the building was occupied and then destroyed sometime before the Civil War, a much earlier date than known to be the case. This date would not be inconsistent with the small quantities of whiteware found in these two deposits (1 out of 250 sherds, or 0.4 percent, in the occupation debris and 35 out of 718, or 4.9 percent, in the destruction debris).

Both the mean occupation and the destruction dates would be misleading if it were not known that the building stood far longer than the dates would imply. This leads to a belief that the use of the building shifted before the Civil War and the dates probably reflect the changing use pattern of the building rather than its demise. This assumption is supported by the photographic evidence which shows that the exterior stairs of the building were removed by the 1870s, and that it had fallen into disrepair and was perhaps being used for some sort of storage. The recovered information supports this assumption. It will be of interest to compare the results of the excavation of the south flanker with those of the north one, which has a known destruction date of 1886.

INVESTIGATION OF THE SOUTH FLANKER AND HOUSE CONNECTION

Following the excavation of the south flanker, it was decided to continue work on the southern side of the main house in an effort to determine the manner of connection between the flanker and the house. An early 18th-century architectural sketch of the house and flankers shows a large colonnade connecting the house to a flanker of considerably grander scale than was ever constructed. Since the flanker size was reduced, it was believed that the colonnade would also have been reduced or altered. As mentioned previously, a line of brick, thought to be part of the connection, was uncovered in the northeast corner of Unit 22 leading from the flanker toward the main house. An 1845 sketch by Lewis Gibbes, a grandson of John Drayton and a professor at the College of Charleston, shows that the connector was brick, about two courses high, topped by a wrought-iron fence (fig. 18). It ran from the northeast corner of the flanker to the southwest corner of the main house without a break.

Two perpendicular trenches, (Units 32-37) two and a half-feet wide, set at 45° angles to the main grid system, were laid out between the flanker and the house in an effort to verify the nature and direction of the connector (Unit 36, fig. 2). A line of half bricks, two courses wide and one course deep, was discovered in the trench running on the northwest-southeast axis (Unit 36). Units 41 and 42 were opened to the north and south of Unit 36 to reveal the wall in its entirety (fig. 19). In many areas the wall had been seriously damaged by tree root growth. Enough of the wall remained intact, however, to afford a determination of its curvature and direction. The Gibbes sketch (fig. 18) appears to be accurate. The remaining wall foundation is largely unmortared and only two courses wide, a width that would be sufficient to support an iron fence. Unfortunately, no evidence of iron work was recovered.

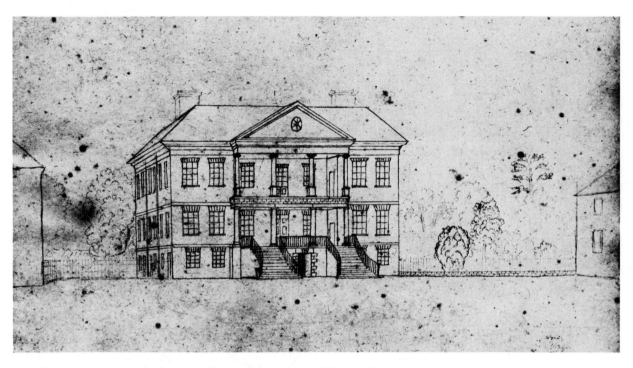

Figure 18: Sketch by Professor Lewis Gibbes of connector between main house and south flanker. (Courtesy of Frank Drayton)

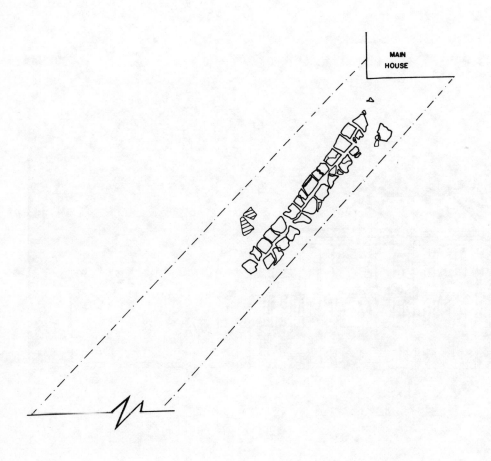

Figure 19

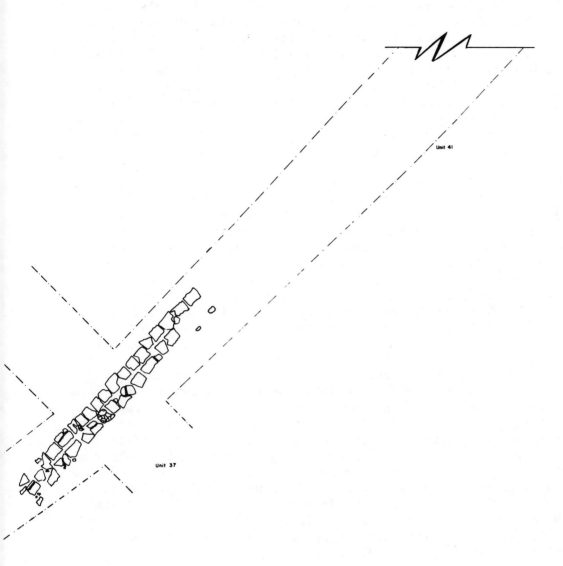

Unit 41

Unit 37

0 .5 1   2   3

N

Bottom course brick

Top course brick

Paving stone

PLAN VIEW, CONNECTOR

Judging from the fact that the connecting wall is not joined to either the flanker or the main house but instead butts into them, it seems likely that the wall was built after the two buildings. There was no builder's trench discernible for the wall, thus making determination of its construction date difficult. It is also not known when the wall was removed, but it does not appear in any of the post-Civil War photographs of the house and flankers. The presence of one sherd of whiteware would indicate that the wall area was still exposed as late as c. 1820, and probably until the Civil War. This is consistent with the information from the south flanker, including a mean ceramic date of 1785.1 (Appendix D, table 5) for the sherds found in association with the wall, and seems to indicate that the wall was removed at about the same time that the flanker's use changed.

The excavation of Units 32-35 was continued and as digging moved closer to the house the amount of household refuse increased. In Unit 35, which abuts the house, the drip line (35C) and a drain area (35F) were excavated. The house foundation spreads three courses before terminating, and at the base of this flare an area of brickbats, laid flat and regularly, was discovered (fig. 20). The west and south boundaries were uncovered and it seems that the whole would measure about 1-1/2 by 3 feet if it were totally exposed. A hole packed with artifacts was excavated—the hole into which a downspout was inserted. This was confirmed by the presence, directly over the area, of brackets for now-absent downspouts and the clear scars on the building where they once were located.

Excavation of Unit 36 revealed an area of considerable interest consisting of a heavy layer of mortar over a level of brick. Beneath the brick was a level of clay fill. The feature contained numerous oyster shells, bone fragments and some green bottle glass. In addition, almost half of an octagonal white salt-glazed stoneware teapot with relief decoration was recovered (fig. 21). The teapot handle was found when another segment of this area, Unit 41, was opened. The handle is of a type that was common on Thomas and John Wedgwood salt-glazed tea wares during the period 1740-50: a handle with two small notches removed from the upper portion to form two flat surfaces. (A similar teapot, attributed to John and Thomas Wedgwood, is illustrated by Mountford [1973:213].) The base of a delft ointment pot with pedestal-foot was recovered but was in extremely poor condition.

Excavation of Unit 36 also revealed a large pit containing what appeared to be raw brick clay. Material of composition identical to this clay, dried and tempered with fiber, was found in the main house. It was used as chinking between the bricks of the walls and was found loose in the attic over the plaster ceiling and in one of the window seats on the second floor. It is probable that these two deposits represented a materials staging area (fig. 22) for the construction of the connecting wall or possibly for repairs to the main house. The features are almost equidistant from the house and the flanker and are about 10 feet from the wall. There were several sherds of pearlware in these deposits, including two of the annular pearlwares, providing a terminus post quem of 1790, making it improbable that they would be associated with the construction of either the house or the flanker. The proximity of the materials staging area to the connecting wall would point to an association with that feature, but does not preclude the possibility that it was associated with house repairs, which were often noted in Charles Drayton's diaries of the time.

51

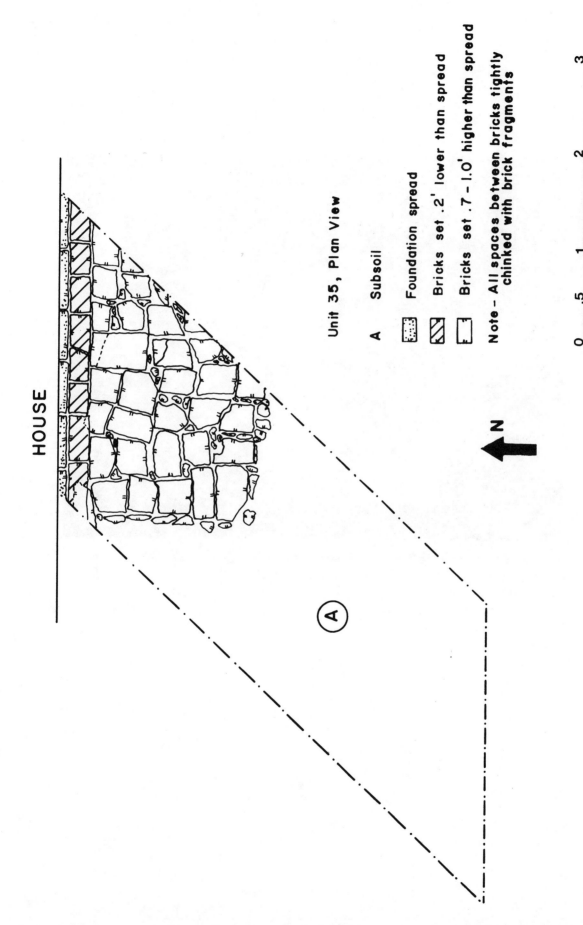

Unit 35, Plan View

A   Subsoil

▨ Foundation spread

▩ Bricks set .2' lower than spread

▢ Bricks set .7 - 1.0' higher than spread

Note - All spaces between bricks tightly chinked with brick fragments

HOUSE

N

feet
0 .5 1 2 3

Figure 20

52

Figure 21: White salt-glazed stoneware octagonal teapot (T. and J. Wedgwood?), 4-1/4" high, excluding handle, Units 36A, 36B, 36C and 41D.

53

UNIT 41, Northwest Profile

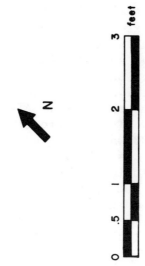

N

0   .5   1   2   3
feet

A Dark brown sandy loam (Topsoil)

B Mortar with occasional brick fragments

C Dark brown sandy loam mottled with 40% orange brown sandy clay & numerous
   brick bats

D Light gray clay mottled with 15% yellow brown marl nodules

E Dark yellow brown sandy clay with 10% marl nodules (Subsoil)

llh
6-20-76

Figure 22

A large triangular unit was opened next to the house. This excavation was prompted by the quantities of household debris found near the house and was undertaken to determine if there was a second drain along this side of the house (there was a second downspout). Units 34 and 35 formed one leg, the house the second and a line between the southwest corner of the house and the southwest corner of Unit 34 formed the third leg. After the sod and topsoil were removed, this area (Unit 38) was divided into six 5-foot-wide subunits perpendicular to the house. Level 38B was excavated maintaining these subdivisions for use in analysis of the distribution of artifacts. Heavy concentrations of household debris, including ceramics, table, window and bottle glass, bones, nails, clay pipes, and such personal items as buttons, straight pins and glass beads were discovered in this area. There were also furniture hardware, harness ornaments and kitchen utensils. Directly beneath this deposit was the level of old topsoil (38N), which was partially excavated and found to be largely undisturbed.

In addition to this area, the drip line (38C) and a trench dug for termite extermination (38D) were excavated (fig. 23). The drip line contained a large quantity of artifacts and the upper levels were heavily mottled with small flecks of red paint which came from the tin roof. The archaeological evidence indicates that the location of the drip line never changed and thus pointed to the fact that the roof shape and pitch has always been the same. This is confirmed by the architectural evidence found in the attic (Chase, personal communication) and by the early photographs and sketches available.

Beneath the disturbed termite trench (38D) was a continuation of the household debris found in 38B, which in turn overlay the builder's trench. At this point the builder's trench was so narrow (1 to 2 inches wide) that it was impractical to excavate.

A large rectangular intrusion was uncovered below the trash deposit (38B) in the eastern portion of the triangle immediately beneath the area where the downspout was. It was thought this would be a drain similar to the one previously uncovered, but excavation revealed that this was not the case. At a depth of 3.5 feet, a large wrought-iron crow's foot lightning rod ground was discovered (fig. 24). It consisted of a V-shaped portion horizontal to the earth and one rod rising perpendicular to the V. The perpendicular portion had been visible since the excavation of 38B began and was joined to the V in what appeared to be a ball and socket joint. The V measures 4 by 4 feet and the perpendicular was 4 feet long. This feature contained predominantly white salt-glazed stoneware chamber pot fragments (72 out of 112 fragments) and dates from 1777.1, using the mean ceramic dating formula (Appendix D, table 6), however, the presence of two transfer-printed pearlware sherds in the assemblage provides a terminus post quem of 1795 for the feature. It was clearly not contemporary with the construction of the main house and is probably associated with repairs or alterations made to the building. Future excavations should be conducted along the northern portion of the house to determine whether there is a similar feature along that side.

It is probable that this area represents repairs or alterations to the building since the feature did cut through all but the uppermost occupational debris. A note found in the diary of Charles Drayton may explain the area: "Waters at D.h. [sic.] higher than has been known since 1752. It rose to the foot of the pigeon house. So that a broad river seemed to [flow] between the dwelling & the hill. The roof of the house much injured many panes of glass broken."

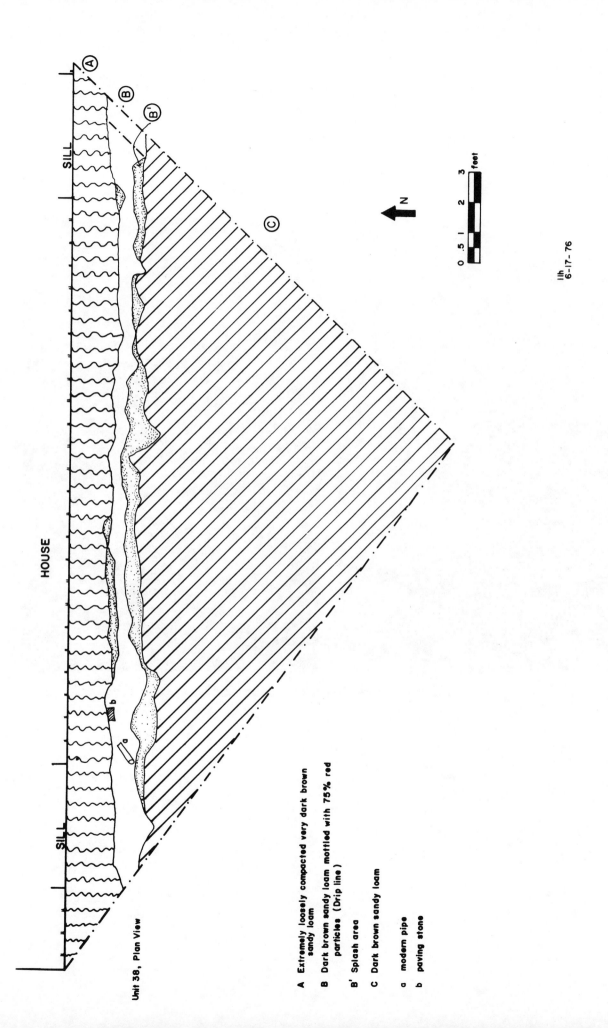

HOUSE

SILL

SILL

SILL

Ⓐ

Ⓑ

Ⓑ'

Ⓒ

N

0 .5 1   2   3
            feet

llh
6-17-76

Unit 38, Plan View

A Extremely loosely compacted very dark brown
   sandy loam

B Dark brown sandy loam mottled with 75% red
   particles (Drip line)

B' Splash area

C Dark brown sandy loam

a modern pipe

b paving stone

Figure 23

Figure 24: Left, lightning rod ground, Unit 38J; right, detail of joint.

(Drayton, 27, 30 August 1813). Thus, roof repairs may have been made at this time and lightning rods added. Benjamin Franklin was among the foremost proponents of the use of lightning rods and they were quickly adopted in the United States. Indeed, by 1772 the lightning rod was evidently such a common feature on American buildings that Franklin commented on their lack in England (Boorstin 1958:257-8).

LAWN TEST EXCAVATIONS

On completion of excavation of this area and concurrently with some of the flanker excavations, several test areas around the lawn were explored. Unit 12 was opened in the hope of finding the structure associated with the destruction debris found in Units 10 and 11, but time did not permit completion of the work. Similarly, excavation of Unit 28, south of the flanker, was not completed. It was hoped that a large depression found there would prove to be a well; however, determination of this will have to await future explorations.

Two units were put in immediately east of the Victorian cottage in an effort to determine if another building had been located near this site. A map of the Ashley River, c. 1850, indicates that Drayton Hall had two flankers and a smaller building to the northeast of the north flanker. The two units were placed in an area that had a concentration of artifacts on the surface and a number of regularly spaced bricks. The brick proved to be a recent fireplace for burning household trash but a structure was not located. More extensive testing both under and around the cottage would be necessary before ruling out a building altogether.

Unit 45 was opened to explore a serpentine line that appeared between the set of brick pillars in front of the east facade of the house and the first drainage ditch, a span of approximately 300 yards, (fig. 2). In his diary for 8 January 1799, Charles Drayton mentions the construction of a 290-foot-long ha-ha and it was thought that the feature might be this ornamental ditch. The feature did not appear until the end of a six-week drought, when the grass growing within the serpentine turned distinctly brown while the surrounding grass remained slightly green. A 2-foot-wide test trench was placed perpendicular to the serpentine and revealed a series of lenticular fills making up the feature (fig. 25). It was probably a Victorian-period flower bed and, indeed, in the spring of 1975 bulbs were still blooming in this area. The feature itself was not wide enough or properly banked to be the ha-ha. An insufficient number of artifacts were recovered to enable any dating.

Finally, a trash dump, located in the woods off the south edge of the lawn, that dated from between the last quarter of the 19th century and the first quarter of the 20th was excavated and dated. It contained numerous bottles, some ceramics, tire tread, a tricycle frame and many unidentifiable iron fragments. A German bisque doll's head with a blown glass eye was also recovered (fig. 26).

EXCAVATION RESULTS

At first glance, the results of the excavation led to the impression that the property saw its heaviest use between 1750 and 1850. For example, a median

58

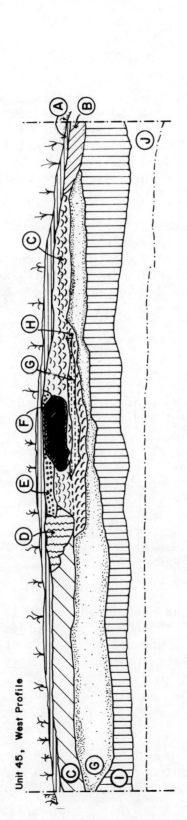

Unit 45, West Profile

A Dark brown sandy loam (Topsoil)
B Dark reddish brown sandy loam
C Dark grayish brown sandy loam
D Very dark brown sandy loam
E Light reddish gray clayey loam
F Light gray – brown clayey loam (Serpentine)
G Dark yellow – brown clayey loam mottled with 10% tan – brown clayey loam
H Dark grayish brown sandy loam mottled with 20% dark yellow – brown
   clayey loam
I Very dark gray – brown sandy loam
J Light gray clay mottled with 15% orange – brown marl nodules

Figure 25

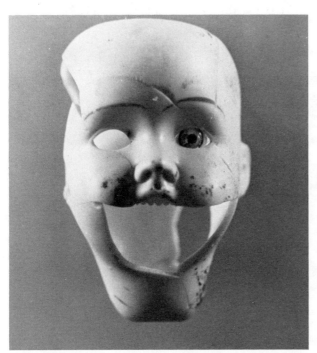 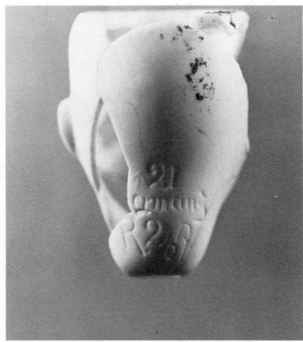

Figure 26: Front and rear views of German-made bisque doll's head (4-1/2"
high), with blown glass eye; ditch trash dump.

date of 1793.9 was calculated for the ceramics from the occupational debris
found along the house by using the mean ceramic dating formula (Appendix D,
table 7, and tables 8-23). This impression is misleading, however, because
the garbage disposal methods evidently altered during the course of occupation.
Those areas nearest the main house do give the earliest dates, but farther
from the house toward the woods, the contents of the trash immediately off
the lawn are of late 19th to early 20th-century origin, with a few containing
trash from the mid-20th century. This observation should lead the archaeologist to exercise a degree of caution when attempting to date the usage span of
one structure solely from debris deposited immediately around the main
structures.

An archaeological project cannot be considered complete without the identification, analysis and interpretation of the recovered artifacts. This process
is especially important at Drayton Hall because it is the first major South
Carolina plantation to have been archaeologically investigated.

Artifacts must be analyzed and interpreted as well as identified. Questions
must be asked of the data to go beyond a simple catalogue of the materials recovered. The artifacts must be tied to those social, economic and utilitarian
factors that made possible their presence on the plantation. The search for
patterns in the life of any given period is vital, and it must be realized that
the archaeological record can provide insights into such patterns. The following questions were basic to the analysis of the artifacts:

1. Does the artifact assemblage as a whole reflect the ongoing history of the
region, and of the Drayton family in particular?

2. What do the artifacts reveal about the lifestyle of the occupants of
Drayton Hall, and how do they augment the documentary record?

In regard to these questions it should be recalled that the Draytons, like so
many other families in Charleston, lost a great many papers during the Civil War.
The public documents that survive are sketchy at best and are particularly poor
for the side of the family that owned Drayton Hall. Inventories do not exist
for any of the owners of Drayton Hall, the closest such documents being a
receipt from Charles Drayton to his father's widow for those possessions of
which she was allowed to retain use during her lifetime and a bill of sale
covering items sold by John Drayton to Thomas Ladson (Appendix B).

There are only a few known pieces of Drayton family furniture, and aside from
the receipt just mentioned, virtually nothing is known about the manner in
which the family lived. It is assumed that they would have lived much as
their relatives and neighbors did. While the archaeological record will not
place furniture back in the house, it will give good indication as to what
household items were in use and what personal adornments were to be found.

3. Can a detailed analysis of the ceramics provide insight into stylistic
patterns?

The history of stylistic change in ceramics is well established for the eastern
United States, but an analysis of the ceramics from Drayton Hall may illustrate
either an adherence to or deviation from this pattern.

4. Can the wealth of the family or other economic factors be determined from
the artifacts?

5. What patterns of property and structure usage can be determined from a
distributional analysis of the artifacts? Do patterns of garbage disposal
follow those discovered on other Anglo-American sites? Are particular travel
patterns discernible and can architectural details be determined from such an
analysis?

With these questions in mind, the more than 83,000 recovered artifacts were
divided into three main groups: prehistoric, trade and historic. The artifacts were then subdivided into six major classes according to function:
(1) household equipment, (2) personal items, (3) construction materials, (4)
labor and technological tools, (5) subsistence items and (6) miscellaneous
items. The artifacts were then further subdivided on the basis of purpose.

PREHISTORIC ARTIFACTS

The prehistoric artifacts recovered from this site are predominantly ceramics,
although numerous flaked chert and jasper pebbles were found, along with two
quartzite projectile points (one each from Unit 2B and Unit 34B). A flint
scraper was recovered from Unit 2F. Most of the Indian pottery dates from the
Savannah, or most recent prehistoric, period (Jean Wardell, personal communication). These ceramics were tempered with grit or sand, but a few shell-
tempered sherds were recovered. Eight types of ceramic were found: (1) plain;
(2) check; (3) simple and (4) complicated stamped; (5) cord and (6) fabric
impressed; (7) punctated; and (8) appliqued (fig. 27).

TRADE ARTIFACTS

Trade artifacts are made up exclusively of Colono-Indian ceramics, which
appear throughout the entire site. This ware is usually untempered although
lightly sand-tempered types do appear. Very few restorable vessels were recovered, making it difficult to determine vessel forms, although the majority
appear to have been hemispherical bowls. Two fragments of special interest
were recovered, one bearing the initials MHD incised into the surface (Maria
Henrietta Drayton was the daughter of Charles Drayton) and the other a small,
shallow, crude pie plate (fig. 28). In all, more than 1,600 sherds of Colono-
Indian ware were recovered. A small number of these sherds were decorated with
red sealing wax, a material used for painted decoration by the Catawba Indians
(Baker 1972:14). Examples of this red-painted ware are also found at Fort
Moultrie in a late 18th-century context (South 1974:185) (fig. 29).

Ivor Noel Hume and others suggest that Colono-Indian ware was purchased for
use by slaves (Noel Hume 1962:172; Baker 1972:14), while some postulate that
persons of the lower socioeconomic strata as well as the slaves were using
this type of ceramic (South 1974:187-8). The locations and context of the
Colono-Indian ceramics recovered from Drayton Hall suggest, however, an
expanded interpretation of their use. While it is reasonably certain that the
slaves would indeed have been using this ware for their own households, there
is far too much found in the immediate vicinity of the house and flanker to
indicate this was its sole function. Evidently, the ware was also purchased
for use in the kitchen of the main house and flanker. While only a few sherds
were recovered from the driveway and mound excavations, more than 400 sherds
came from the trash heap, and the balance, more than 1,000, were found in the
occupation and destruction levels of the south flanker and the occupation
level of the main house. Only eight of these sherds were recovered in the
construction levels; so, although the labor force (presumably slaves) could
have deposited some, that does not account for this great quantity of Colono-
Indian ware. It is apparent that even a wealthy household made use of these
readily available and inexpensive goods.

Figure 27: Prehistoric Indian unglazed earthenware. Top row, left to right: stamped, Unit 32C/BR; complicated stamped, Unit 20G/AA; and cord impressed, Units 36B/BL and 20D/AD. Second row, all stamped, Units 31AA, AB, AC, AD, 37C/AA, 17L/AH. Third row, first two sherds appliqued, Units 38B IVa/OR, 37D/BR; third and fourth sherds, punctated, Units 38B Va/AR and AS. Lower right, pinched design, Unit 22J/AA and punctated, Unit 17B/CV.

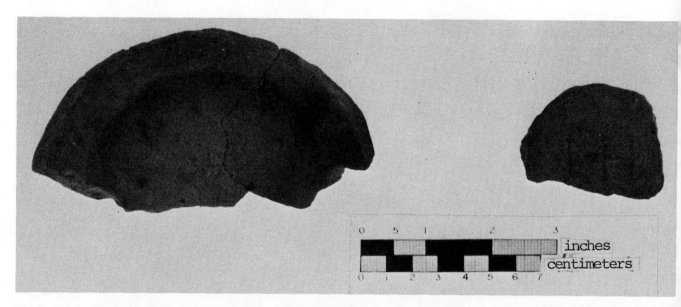

Figure 28: Colono-Indian unglazed earthenware. Left, fragment of a plate similar to a pie plate, Unit 41D; right, sherd with initials <u>MHD</u> incised into surface, Unit 22B/GD.

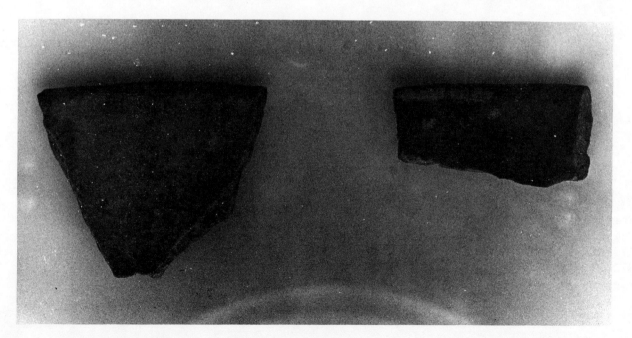

Figure 29: Colono-Indian unglazed earthenware, red wax decorated (scale 1:4), Unit 11B/AA and AQ.

It is entirely possible that the Colono-Indian ware was being manufactured
on the plantation or very near by. Although there is no inventory for John
or Charles Drayton, Stephen Fox Drayton (John's brother) had 31 Indians listed
in his inventory (Wills, 1734). In the 1792 census for St. Andrew's Parish,
of which Drayton Hall is a part, there are 31 persons listed under the category
"all other free persons," while in the 1800 census there are three persons
listed under "all other free persons except Indians." On the basis of the
exclusion of Indians in the 1800 census, it is possible to argue that there
were as many as 28 Indians accounted for in the 1792 census. Another indicator
that this ware was being manufactured nearby or on the plantation is the
fragment found with the initials MHD on it; Maria Henrietta Drayton did reside
at Drayton Hall from the late 1780s until the 1840s. Further proof that this
ware was in use for a long period of time is the fact that it was found in
the construction levels and throughout the destruction levels, which have a
terminus post quem of c. 1820, based on the presence of several sherds of
whiteware.

HISTORIC PERIOD ARTIFACTS

Household Equipment

It should be noted that common household objects rather than fine or purely
decorative items are more likely to be found in an archaeological site (Noel
Hume 1962:169). Ornamental items would have been better cared for and passed
on from generation to generation and thus most likely would not be found at
a site. Purely decorative items were generally scarce, particularly during
the colonial period. A recent study of ceramics in Philadelphia between 1780
and 1800 reveals only eight references to ornamental objects in the inventories
of this period, with only two stating specifically what these objects were:
some "Mandarine figures" in Benjamin Franklin's inventory and a "Sett of
Derbyshire Ornaments" in the inventory of sea captain Peter Odlin (Gill 1976:
88-9).

Ceramics. The ceramics recovered from the Drayton Hall excavations show a
broad range, both in date and style, varying from the crudest earthenwares to
the finest overglaze enameled porcelains. Ceramic fragments appeared in all
areas investigated, although the largest quantities came from the vicinity of
the main house and the south flanker. Divided on the basis of fine ware
versus kitchenware, there were 7,225 sherds of fine ware, representing almost
68 percent of the historic period ceramics recovered. Of the kitchenware
(3,295 sherds), almost half were Colono-Indian ceramics. Detailed identification of the historic period ceramics recovered at Drayton Hall is contained
in Appendix F.

The preponderance of tablewares over kitchenwares (68 percent versus 32 percent) is unusual. No complete vessels were recovered, nor was it possible to
completely restore any. This heavy fragmentation is most likely due to the
fact that the excavations were conducted in trash and destruction areas
rather than wells or privies, where the potential for finding complete
vessels is greater.

Glass. Under domestic items, the glass was divided into two categories: bottle
and table. Dark green bottle glass (wine bottles), pharmaceutical bottle glass,

case bottle glass and various table glass vessels were found in the course of the excavations. Indeed, some of the finest pieces of household items were fragments of lead metal table glass.

Charles Drayton makes frequent references to his wine bottling and storage activities at Drayton Hall, for example, noting on 24 May 1792 how many bottles of clear wine and how many with "lees" (dregs) he can bottle from a particular cask of wine or noting how long he has aged a wine. Of the 9,452 bottle glass fragments found, more than 7,000 (76.2 percent) were from dark green wine bottle or case bottles. The bottle shapes ranged in date from approximately the second quarter of the 18th century to the mid-19th century. One identifiable Dutch bottle neck and one American bottle were recovered, along with fragments of several case (square) bottles of both green and blue metal. There were no complete wine bottles (fig. 30) recovered, nor were there enough fragments of sufficient completeness to allow the application of Carillo's dating formula (Carillo 1974).

A number of pharmaceutical bottle fragments were recovered (fig. 31), many dating from the last half of the 18th century, along with several molded examples from the second quarter of the 19th century. The trash pit in the drainage ditch contained large quantities of late 19th to early 20th-century patent medicine bottles.

The majority of the table glass was recovered from the area just outside the house where there was a wide variety of vessel forms, including decanter, wine glass, stopper, plate, bowl, candlestick, compote and tumbler fragments, many of which were of lead metal. Datable wine glass stems, including several fragments of air twist stems (fig. 32) ranged from 1735 to 1775, and a faceted decanter stopper dates from c. 1760.

Cooking and Eating Utensils. In comparison to the vast quantities of glass and ceramics found on the site, the number of cooking and eating utensils recovered was quite limited. Much of the iron recovered from the site was in a highly deteriorated condition and could not be identified. Three iron two-tined forks dating from the mid-18th century were recovered. Only five spoon fragments, one an iron bowl and two white metal spoon handle fragments were found. There was only one identifiable knife fragment. A few fragments of heavy cast-iron cooking pots were found. Partial bone handles from two forks were recovered, one with a brass rivet still in place (fig. 33).

Furniture Hardware. Several pieces of brass furniture hardware were recovered, including one whole and one restorable back plate (escutcheon) for a drawer pull, two screw-ended posts with nuts for the drawer pull and one whole and one partial bail. The whole plate, the posts and bail all fit together and date from the third quarter of the 18th century (fig. 34).

A small marble column, approximately five inches high and one inch in diameter, was found. While its function has not been definitely determined, it is hypothesized that this was an ornamental section for a mantle or table clock. Two other clock parts were also found, although these probably belonged to a tall case or "grandfather" clock. The first is a segment of a brass clock face showing the symbol II with what appears to be the number 10 above (fig. 35). From the placement of a tiny triangular pointer between the 10 and the II, it would seem that the symbol II was used for each hour, with the appropriate number being placed above. A second item is thought to be a key for

-Text continues on page 75

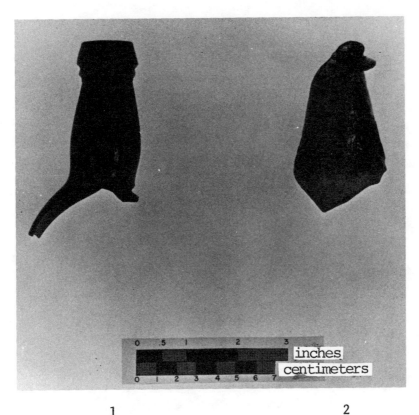

1   2

Figure 30: Dark green wine bottle necks. (1) from
Unit 37B, (2) from 11B/YB. Next pages (3) from
Unit 22B/BOU, (4) 10A/RI; (5) Unit 38B IIIa/WM,
(6) 22B/BOT. (7-10, 13, 14) bottle bases of dark
green wine bottle glass; (11) case bottle glass;
light green metal; (12) clear bottle glass ; (7)
Unit 22B/BRX; (8) 22B/BRJ (2" maximum height);
(10) 36A/AB; (11) 35B/AYZ; (12) 10A/QT (3-1/2"
maximum width); (13) 38B IVa/ON; (14) 41E/AB
(4-5/8" maximum width).

-Continued on next page

3   4

5   6

-Continued on next page

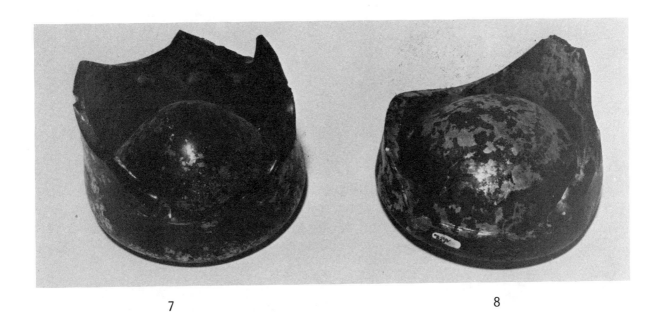

7   8

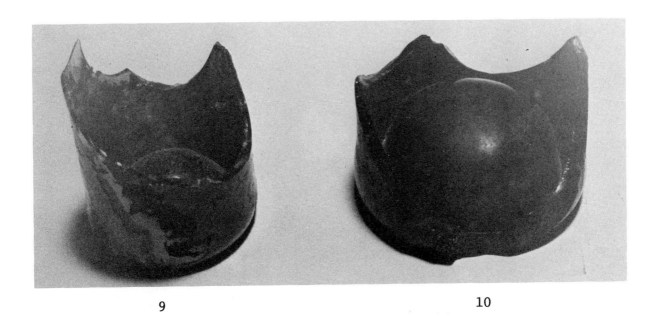

9   10

-Continued on next page

11
12

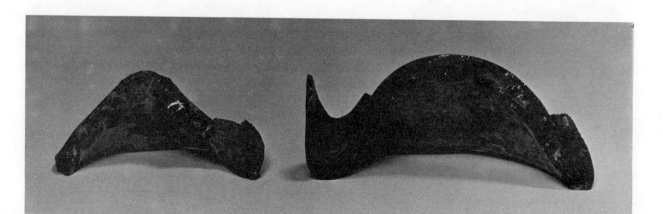

13
14

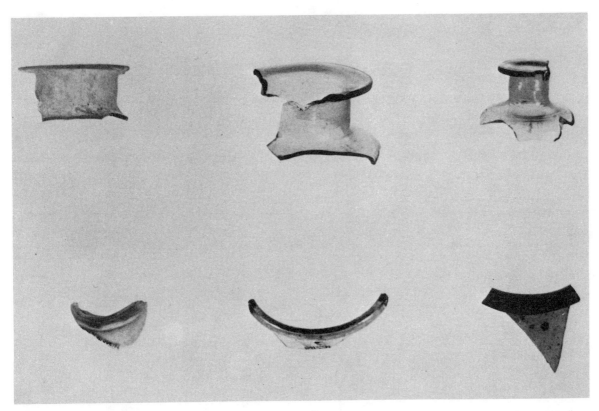

Figure 31: Pharmaceutical bottle necks. Top row, left, clear metal; others, light green metal; neck in middle, top row, measures 1-7/8" across; Units 33B/AES, 38L/HX, 35D/HE, 38B IIIa/WQ, 4C/CE, 35B/AYW.

72

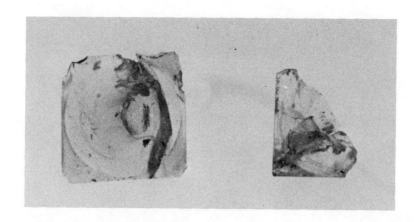
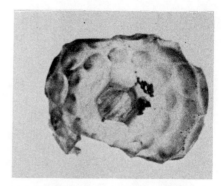

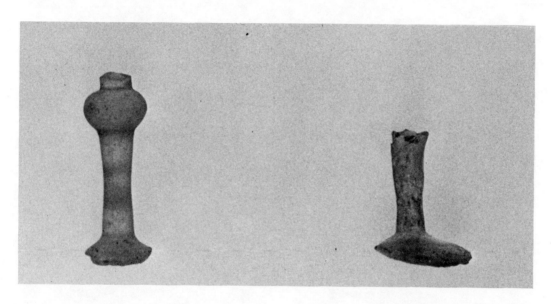

Figure 32: Table glass. Upper left photo: candlestick bases, clear
metal, Units 35B/BFJ, 38B IIIa/VQ, VR (2-1/8" square). Upper right
photo: goblet bowl, Unit 38L/HH, HK, (2-1/4" maximum width). Middle: wine glass stems, clear metal; left, plain, Unit 34B/BUV (2-
3/4" high); right, faceted, Unit 22B/ATC. Lower photo: wine glass
stems, clear metal with air twist; left, Unit 38B IIIa/VP (1-1/4"
high); right, Unit 38B IVa/NS.

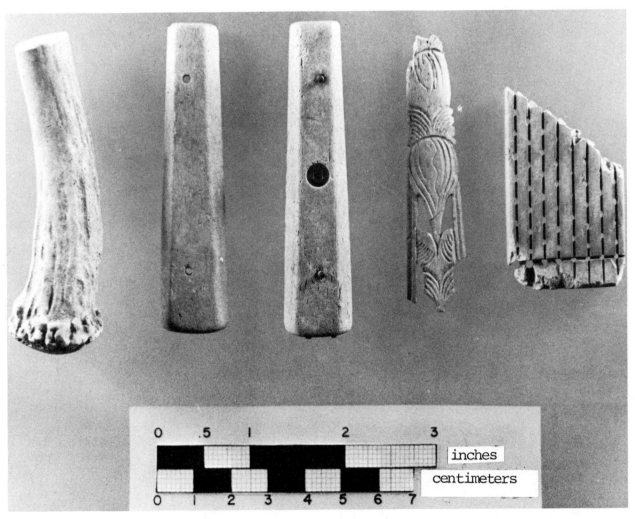

Figure 33: Worked bone. Left to right: antler handle, Unit 17B/ZS; bone handle, Unit 38B/VIS; bone handle, Unit 34B/BUR; bone fan handle, Unit 20E/JV; bone brush back, Unit 38H/US.

Figure 34: Brass furniture hardware. Top row: back plates (whole plate measures 3-9/16" across), Units 22B/DKQ, DKP, DKR, 38B III. Bottom row: bail, Unit 38B IVa and nut and screw threaded mounting post, Unit 22B. The broken plate and mounting post evidently are from the same piece of furniture. The bail fits the post and may also be from the same piece, although it was found at a distance from the other two pieces.

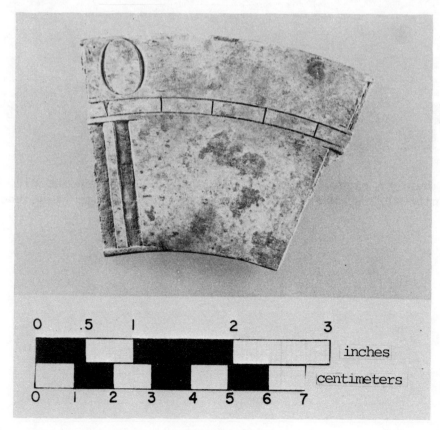

Figure 35: Brass clock face fragment, Unit 37D.

winding up the weights of a tall case clock. It is brass, with a square end to fit into the keyhole, the balance being a C curve with a brass finial at the end.

Sewing Equipment. Sewing implements, such as pins and thimbles, have been included under household equipment. A total of five brass or white metal thimbles was recovered, all of two-piece construction and ranging in size from 5/8 inch high by 5/8 inch across the opening to what may be a child's thimble measuring 7/16 inch high by 1/2 inch across the opening. A total of 17 straight pins was recovered, all of brass and all with spun heads. The largest was 1-3/8 inches long and 3/64 inch wide, while the smallest measured 1-3/8 inches long and 1/32 inch wide. Only two other pins were complete, both measuring 1-3/8 inches long by 1/32 inch across (fig. 36). All the other pin fragments were also 1/32 inch across. Several brass rings, possibly used as curtain rings were also found (fig. 37). In addition, two lead finials were found; the function of these has not been determined.

Personal Items

Those items found in a household that would most likely have been in the possession of one person for exclusive use, rather than for the benefit of the household in general, have been termed personal items.

Tobacco Pipes. Certainly the most common personal possession was the clay tobacco pipe. These were generally made of white clay and imported from England, Scotland, Holland or France. All countries of manufacture but Holland were represented at Drayton Hall. A few pipes of apparently North American manufacture are also included in the assemblage.

During the course of the Drayton Hall excavations, more than 440 pipe stem fragments were recovered; of these only 14 were decorated. In addition, 19 plain and 3 decorated pipe stems that were elliptical in cross section were found. These came from pipes with curved rather than straight stems. One red clay reed pipe stem fragment was recovered, and six stem ends were identified. Of the four marked stems found, two were from McDougal, Glasgow (last half of the 19th century); another is stamped "Morgan" on one side and "Liverpool" on the other side; and the fourth reads "L. Fiolet" in a band circling the stem and has a leaf cartouche encircling the number 945 on one side of the stem (fig. 38). This particular stem is of French origin, from the L. Fiolet Company in St. Omer, France.

Four hundred fifteen plain, undatable pipe bowl fragments were discovered, along with 80 variously decorated bowl fragments and five stoneware bowl fragments. There were 16 bowls or partial bowls large enough for analysis and, of these, 11 were decorated and/or marked (see table 2 for details on the whole and partial bowls). Two of the most interesting bowls recovered were one with a basket-weave pattern covering the entire bowl and another with a skull and crossbones motif on both sides of the bowl with the seam molded to look like rope stitching (fig. 39). The basket-weave bowl is smaller than usual, is of a darker yellowish brown clay and is probably North American in origin. The skull and crossbones bowl most likely dates from the period between 1825 and 1875.

-Text continues on page 83

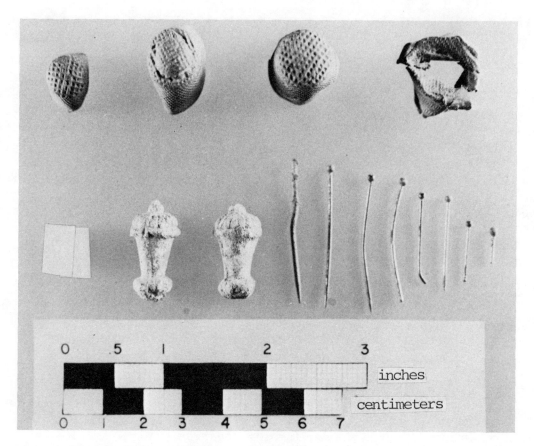

Figure 36: Sewing equipment. Upper row: thimbles, Units 34B, 22B
and 38B IIIa. Bottom row: lead weights, perhaps used as drapery
weights, Units 35D and 38B Va; straight pins; first pin, Unit 4B,
others, Unit 38B IIIa.

Figure 37: Brass
rings. Upper row
from Units 38B IIIa,
38B IVa and 10C/EK;
lower row from Units
38B V, 11C/BEA and
10B/BUQ.

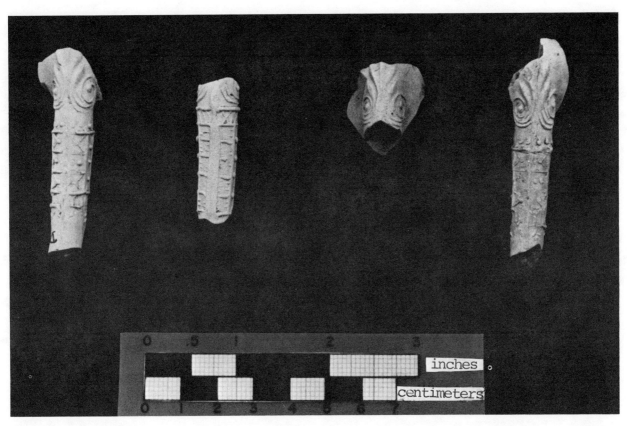

Figure 38: White clay pipe stems. Upper photo: raised molded decoration, Units
17B/ES, ET, 33A/BP, 36B/EE and 39A/CN. Lower photo: L. Fiolet ("945"), 1-1/4"
long, Unit 16B/ER. Next page, upper photo, left to right: ellipsoidal, Unit
17B/EG ET; McDougal, Glasgow, 3-5/8" long, Unit 38H/TP; McDougal, Glasgow, Unit
22B/ABT; Morgan, Liverpool, Unit 38B/GA; terra cotta, Unit 17B/FG; all others,
white clay, Units 38B III/CQ, 38B Va/PI, 10B/ARQ, provenience unknown, 17A/AB,
22N/AEU. Long, white stem end is 2-27/32" long, Unit 38B Va/RJ.

-Continued on next page

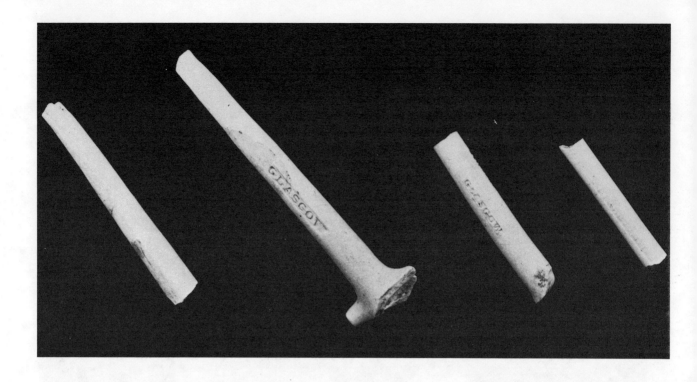

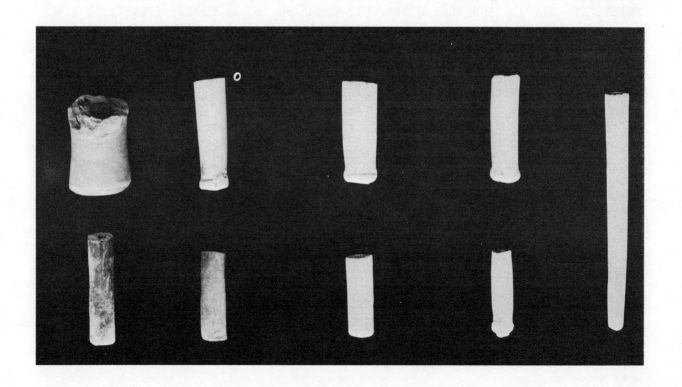

TABLE 2
PIPE BOWLS

Provenince Number	Bore Diameter	Description	Date
DH.34B/BUS	4/64"	Whole bowl, with initials TD stamped on back; number 15 raised on left side of spur.	1st half 19th century
DH.33A/BQ	5/64"	Whole bowl, with base molded to look like a hand; stem molded to look like a sleeve; stem is elliptical and curved.	2nd half 19th century
DH.38BIII/CR	5/64"	Whole bowl, with raised skull and crossbones motif within triangle on both sides of bowl; seam molded to resemble rope stitching; no spur or heel.	1st half 19th century
DH.38BV/IT	5/64"	Whole bowl, with initials TD raised on back; spur.	1820-60
DH.2E/AK	5/64"	Partial bowl, plain with the number 4 stamped on bottom of stem; no spur or heel.	1730-90
DH.2F/DV, DU	5/64"	Partial bowl, plain slightly bulbous body; broken spur.	18th century?
DH.11B/PM	5/65"	Partial bowl, gadrooned; no spur or heel.	1775-1850
DH.38BVI/EU, EV	5/64"	Partial bowl, with initials IC stamped within dashed circle on back of bowl, upside down; no spur or heel.	1775-1800
	5/64"	Partial bowl, with initials R.F. raised on both sides of spur and raised leaves on back seam.	19th century
	5/64"	Two partial bowls, plain; no spur or heel.	1720-1820
DH.38BIVa/NJ	6/64"	Whole bowl, basket weave raised design with gadrooned base, of pinkish-gray body; no spur or heel. (Locally manufactured?)	1790-1820

80

Table 2, continued

DH.32C/CX	6/64"	Whole bowl (small fragment missing), with initials R.T. stamped on back (R. Tippet) and an illegible cartouche on right side. No spur or heel.	1725-75
	6/64"	Partial bowl, plain. No spur or heel.	1720-1820
DH.38BIIa/LF	6/64"	Partial bowl, with initials I.L. stamped on left side (right side of bowl missing).	1725-75
	6/64"	Partial bowl, plain; no spur or heel.	1720-1820

NOTE: In descriptions, positions of marks or decoration based on bowls held in smoking position.

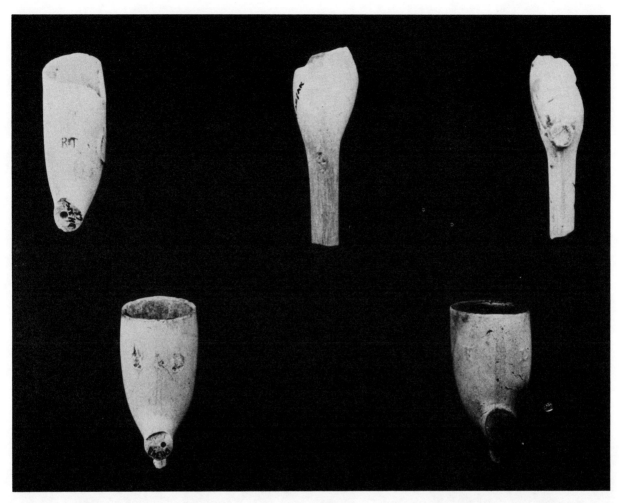

Figure 39: White clay pipe bowls. Upper photo, top row, R. Tippett, Unit 32C/CX; number 4 stamped on base of stem, Unit 2E/AK; plain bowl with spur, Unit 2F/DU, DV; bottom row: T.D. bowl, Unit 34B, T.D. Bowl, Unit 38BV (15/16" exterior bowl diameter). Next page, top photo: left to right: T.C. bowl, Unit 38B VI/EU, EV; gadrooned bowl, Unit 11B/PM; raised molded decoration, Unit 37B; buff clay basket-weave pattern, Unit 38B IVa/NJ (13/16" exterior diameter). Lower photos: skull and crossbones bowl, Unit 38B IIIa/CR; hand motif, Unit 33A;BQ (1" exterior bowl diameter); IL bowl, Unit 38B IIa/LF.

–Continued on next page

82

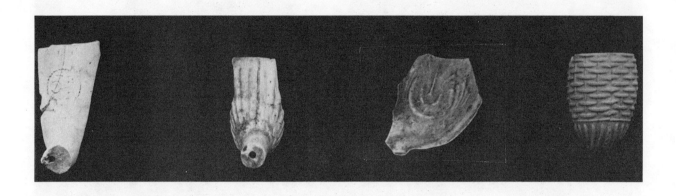

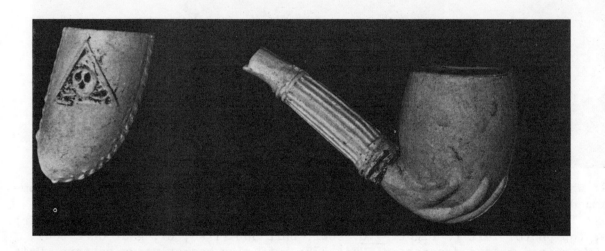

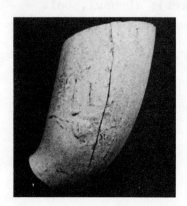

The types of bowl decoration represented are gadroons (23), rouletted lips (3), numbers or initials (6), cross-hatching (2) and, most commonly, raised decorative motifs such as leaves and flowers (46).

The pipe stem dating formula devised by Harrington and modified by Binford (Harrington 1954; Binford 1962) was applied to several areas of excavation, but as has been the case in other excavations of this era, the dates were consistently too early, ranging from 37 to 69 years earlier than dates determined by other means. It should be remembered, though, that the number of pipe stems used (except for the site as a whole) was not sufficient to provide particularly accurate dates (see Appendix G, a separate volume to this report entitled Quantification of Artifacts from the Drayton Hall Excavations.

Clothing. Rarely does the archaeologist find items of clothing preserved, but the more durable portions of a garment, such as buttons or other fasteners, are frequently found. At Drayton Hall these items are represented by buckles, buttons, hooks, grommets and an overalls hitch.

The single overalls hitch recovered is of brass and is stamped "Patent 1855." It is identical to one found in the excavation of a slave cabin at Cannon's Point, St. Simons Island, Ga. (McFarlane 1975). The presence of the hitch near the house raises speculation as to who was wearing the overalls, although it was most likely a slave or one of the squatters known to have occupied the plantation toward the end of the Civil War. An adjusting clamp for suspenders was recovered from the trash pit outside the south flanker.

Several shoe buckles were recovered from the site, some of which were plain and some elaborately decorated. None of the tangs was preserved. Most of the buckles date from the mid-18th century (fig. 40).

Three brass hooks from a hook and eye-type fastener were recovered, along with 12 small copper or copper alloy grommets. The use of the grommets has not been determined, although they are most often found on heavier materials. The most common of the clothes fasteners were buttons (figs. 41, 42, 43) of metal, bone, porcelain and hard rubber. Of the 80 metal buttons, only two were military, one from the 2nd Artillery, dating from the War of 1812; the other, lettered USA on the face, can be attributed to the Continental Army. A detailed description of the buttons follows (based on South's button typology as presented in Noel Hume 1972:90-91):

Type 6 - Metal, with cast face flux joined to cast back. The button is cast with the eye in place, leaving a casting spur. (1 recovered)

Type 7 - Metal, flat cast button with spun back. Button cast with eye in place. (14 recovered)

Type 8 - Metal (brass), cast with mold seam visible on the back. (3 recovered)

Type 9 - Metal (brass), flat disc with hand-stamped face design. Eye soldered to the back and no foot. (14 recovered)

Type 11 - Metal, one piece cast soft white metal with mold seam visible on the back. (2 recovered)

-Text continues on page 88

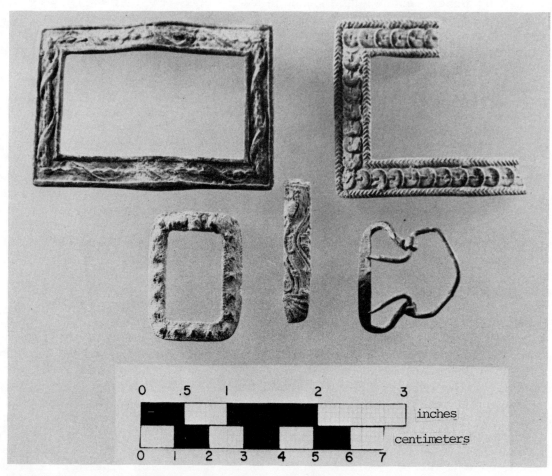

Figure 40: Brass buckles. Top row, shoe buckles; left, from Unit 11B/AXG; right, from Unit 20BE/MR. Bottom row, left to right: clothing buckle, Unit 20E/FY; buckle fragment, Unit 22B/DLD; overalls hitch, Unit 38B V.

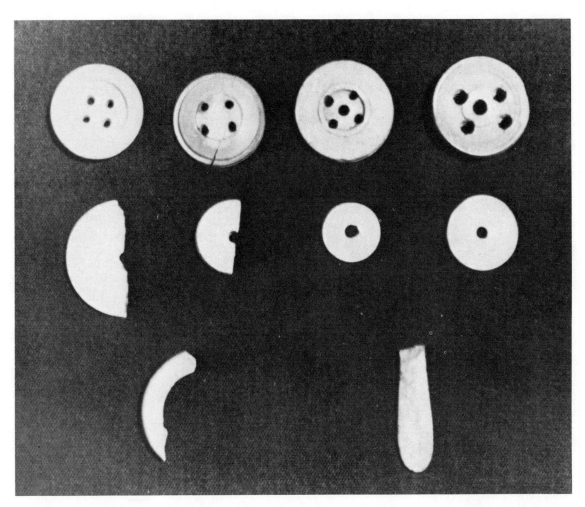

Figure 41: Bone artifacts. Upper row, left to right: four-hole button, type 20, four-hole button, type unknown, Units 38L/IB and 38B III/CT; two five-hole buttons, type 19, Units 22B/BSB, 41C/BP. Middle row, one-hole button backs, type 15, Units 10B/CRL, 22B/BSD, 11C/BYQ, 38B IIIa/WR. Bottom row: bone ring with red painted edge, Unit 22B/BSC; bone stay tip (?), Unit 38B Ia/BE.

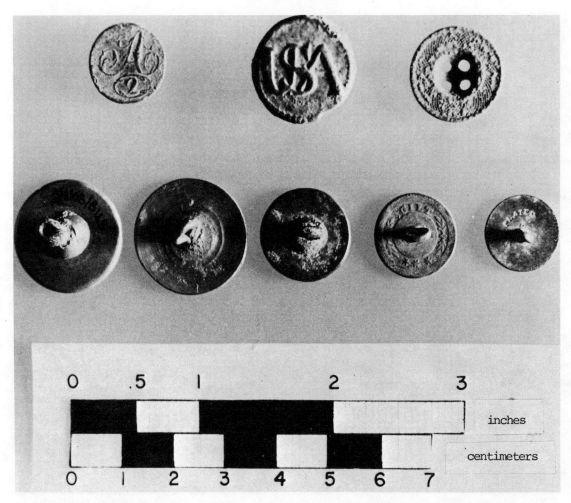

Figure 42: Metal buttons. Upper row, left to right: 2nd Artillery, type 9, Unit 18C/DP; U.S.A., type 11, Unit 10B/BUW; stamped brass, type 32, Unit 38B V/JA. Bottom row, left to right: white metal, type 7, Unit 10B/BUW; brass plated, type 18, Unit 11B/AGV; brass plated, type 18, Unit 11B/AGV.

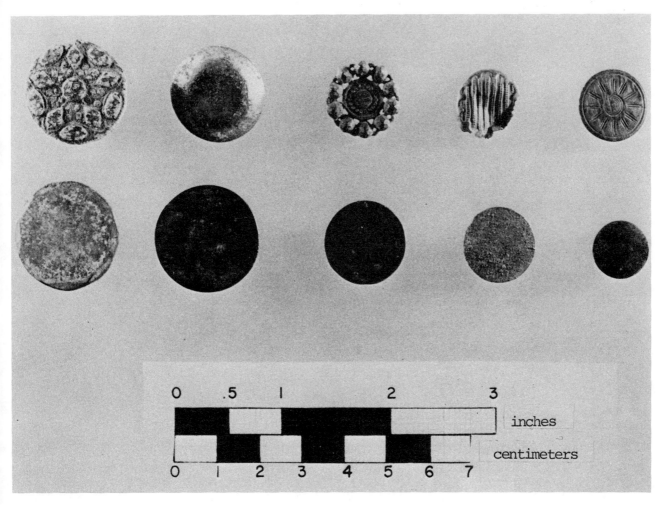

Figure 43: Metal buttons. Upper row, left to right: molded brass, type 9, Unit 17B/PQ, domed brass, type 28, Unit 37B; pierced metal, type 7, Unit 10C/EL. Bottom row, left to right: faceted brass, type 9, Unit 11C/BDT; plain brass, type 7, Unit 11C/BDZ; plain brass, type 7, Unit 38B IVa/OA; plain white metal, type 9, Unit 4C 11/FK; domed brass, type 9, Unit 11B/AGT.

Type 15 - Bone, one-hole bone disc with no off-set rim. (6 recovered)

Type 16 - Metal, flat-back disc with crimped-on rim face and soldered eye. (1 recovered)

Type 17 - Metal, cast pierced brass with casting plugs visible on the back. (1 recovered)

Type 18 - Metal, stamped brass with words and designs on the back. (8 re-covered)

Type 19 - Bone, four-hole bone button with centering, fifth hole, for cutting tool. The back is usually flat. (2 recovered)

Type 20 - Bone, four-hole disc with the back often rounded. (6 recovered)

Type 21 - Metal, four-hole button with an iron face and back; fiber center. (2 recovered)

Type 23 - Porcelain, four-hole button with convex front and back. (35 recovered)

Type 24 - Metal, iron back and front with a loose iron eye through the back, originally fabric covered. (3 recovered)

Type 27 - Metal, domed, machine embossed with the eye loose or soldered in the hole. (1 recovered)

Type 28 - Metal, machine-stamped with a concave back and a poorly soldered eye. (2 recovered)

Type 29 - Metal, cast soft white metal with wire eye cast in large boss.   (3 recovered)

Type 30 - Metal, four-hole button of cast soft white metal. (1 recovered)

Type 32 - Metal, stamped brass, four-hole button with sunken panel for the holes. (6 recovered)

In general, types 6 through 16 date from the period 1726-76; types 17 through 23 from the period 1800-30; and types 7, 11, 15, 16 and 18-32 also occur between 1837 and 1865.

Four sleeve buttons were recovered during the course of the excavations. One was octagonal, brass and solid cast with a decorated face. It probably dates from the first half of the 18th century, measures 3/4 an inch across the face and the eye is drilled through the shank, which was cast as one piece with the button itself. The second sleeve button dates from after the 1770s, is oval (5/8 inch at its widest) and is gilded. Finally, there is a cast white metal sleeve button, the eye and the back one piece, with faceted glass front (fig. 44). The back is domed and the link, also white metal, is still attached.

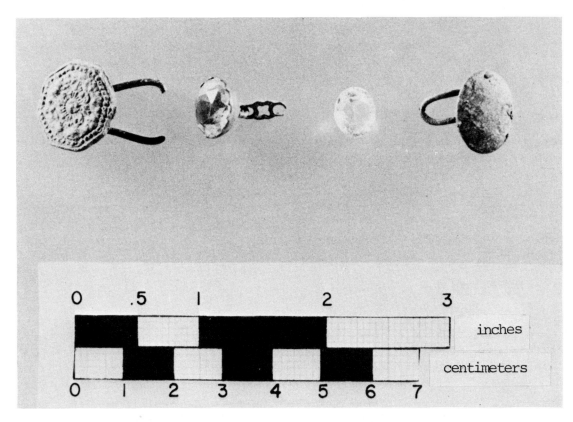

Figure 44: Sleeve buttons. Left to right, octagonal, molded brass, Unit 22B/DLG; faceted glass with white metal back, Unit 38B IIIa; faceted glass rhinestone, Unit 17J/CF; domed brass, Unit 38B IVa.

Sixteen metal buttons of various types that could not be correlated with the South button types were found, including a flat metal (brass?) core with a highly corroded iron oxide (?) coating and enamel on the face over the coating. A bone button back (turned green), similar to type 20, but with two layers of gold leaf over a concave front, was also recovered.

Beads. Thirty-two glass beads, faceted and unfaceted, with colors including red, blue, striped and clear were found in many areas of the site. The beads ranged in date from the late 18th century to the mid-19th century (fig. 45).

Coins. Only five coins were found, three of half-penny denomination. There were two George II (young-head) and one George III (young-head) found (fig. 13). While finding such coins is not unique, what is highly unusual is that all three of these coins were minted in Ireland. None of the dates was legible but all were in the 18th century.

Toys. Five clay marbles were found during the excavations. In the 20th-century dump the bisque doll's head previously mentioned (fig. 26) was found, along with the frame of a tricycle.

Other. A brass pistol butt plate in the shape of an anthropomorphic face (fig. 46) was recovered from the 18th-century trash deposit (10B). It is quite detailed, showing the teeth, pupils of the eyes and a pig-like nose. Several fragments of rectangular graphite pencil were found and half a carved bone fan handle and part of a brush back were excavated (fig. 33).

Construction Material

Window Glass. The single most numerous item excavated was window glass. In all, more than 30,000 fragments of window glass were excavated, 72.3 percent (21,856 fragments) from Unit 38 alone, the triangular unit immediately against the house. This extraordinary amount of window glass is possibly the result of a severe storm that necessitated major roof and window repairs. Charles Drayton did record in his diary (Drayton 27, 30 August 1813) that damage had been done to the roof and window panes were broken. Further, the historical architect confirmed that all the window sashes were changed during the early 19th century. This would make the vast quantities of window glass found outside the house more readily explicable, although it is still possible that the glass derives from some other source. Some of the glass was of more recent date, the result of vandalism or of natural mishaps, but these two factors can account for only a small portion of the window glass fragments found.

Nails and Spikes. More than 14,700 nails and spikes were excavated, including handwrought, machine-cut and wire types, although few of the latter were discovered. A large number of the nails were found in the south flanker area, a result in accordance with the hypothesis that this building was intentionally dismantled. More difficult to account for is the large quantity of nails that was found in the area immediately outside the main house. This may be the result of the window alterations and roof repairs mentioned previously or of the post-Civil War repairs that were made to the house. The majority of the nails were badly corroded.

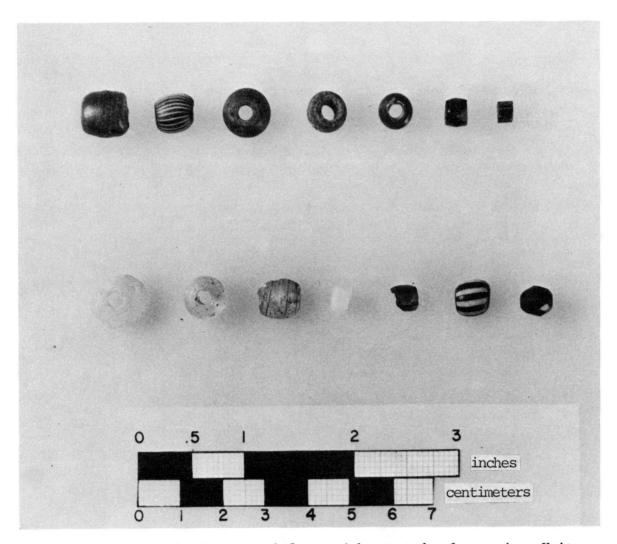

Figure 45: Glass beads. Top row, left to right: wound, ultramarine, Unit 38B V/JG; tubular brite navy with 26 white stripes; wound, brite navy, provenience unknown; wound, brite navy, Unit 17B/SH; wound, brite navy, Unit 22B/BSE; tubular faceted brite navy, Unit 38B IVa/QD; tubular brite navy, Unit 17B/SG. Bottom row: wound, light gold (opal), Unit 22B/BSF; wound, clear crystal, Unit 17B/SE; wound, pale blue (opal), Unit 17B/BJT; tubular white, Unit 7B/GE; tubular, faceted emerald, Unit 18B/OE; tubular, black and white stripes, Unit 17B/SI, tubular, faceted black, Unit 10B/DFO.

92

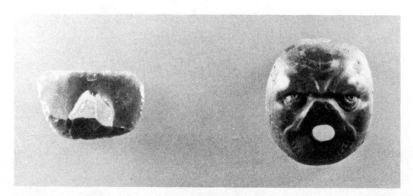

Figure 46: Left, honey color gun flint, Unit 20BE/NF; right, brass pistol butt plate, Unit 10B/BUX (1-3/16" maximum width).

| 0 | .5 | 1 | | 2 | | 3 |
inches
centimeters
| 0 | 1 | 2 | 3 | 4 | 5 | 6 | 7 |

Figure 47: Harness ornaments. Left to right: brass, Unit 34B, lead alloy, Unit 35D, brass, Unit 20E/FX.

In addition to the numerous iron nails and spikes, several brass nails were recovered, principally from the area outside the main house. Such nails were often used when installing slate shingles (brass will not rust and stain the slate), and so it is thought that these nails date to the period of installation of the slate roof on the house.

Building Hardware. Numerous fragments of window and door hardware were discovered, including strap hinges, a shutter pintel, an iron padlock and a brass keyhole escutcheon plate. In addition, three iron keys (one whole and two partial) were recovered.

Several pieces of lead, both flat and resembling caming, also were found. According to the architectural historian, the windows were originally sash type, so that caming would not have originated from casement windows on the main house. It is possible that this was material salvaged from an earlier outbuilding that had casement windows, possibly from a site other than Drayton Hall. The flat lead pieces are more readily explained. These would have been pieces of the lead flashing or guttering that were once on the roof and water tables, portions of which still exist. An analysis of the lead would be required to establish this explanation beyond doubt, but it is certainly the most likely source.

Brick, Plaster and Mortar. Brick rubble was discovered in such large quantities in some areas that it was quantified by cubic feet rather than individually. A total of more than 42 cubic feet (1,274 quarts) of brick was removed from the site, 31.3 cubic feet (947 quarts) from the south flanker alone. In addition, more than 200 brickbats or whole bricks were retained. Numerous pieces of plaster were recovered from the site, some of it finely finished. The majority of the plaster fragments was discovered in the driveway and mound excavation areas. Mortar samples were taken from all areas and then put aside for analysis at a future date. Most of the mortar samples contained traces of oyster shell, which would have been burned and used for its lime content.

Other Building Materials. Large quantities of slate were removed from the site. In the area of the 18th-century trash deposit, more than 0.6 cubic foot (18.5 quarts) of slate were removed. Over the rest of the site a total of 263 whole slates or slate pieces showing a nail hole were preserved. The majority of the slates were found in the area of the main house. The large amount of slate in the trash deposit seems to indicate that the building from which this rubble came once had a slate roof. This indication was further supported by the presence of numerous fragments of roofing tiles. These were not pan tiles, but rounded, or "ridge" tiles used to cover the joints between two angles of the roof, particularly on the peak of a roof.

Several fragments of paving stone, particularly in the area of the south flanker, were recovered from the site, although an almost equal number were found in the 18th-century trash deposit. These stones may have been used to line paths between the various buildings, as the soil around Drayton Hall becomes very sticky and boggy when saturated, which it often is.

A lightning rod ground found along the south facade of the main house has been included with the building materials.

Labor and Technological Tools

One major class of artifact that is not well represented at the site is that of tools. At first glance this does not seem especially remarkable, because most of the excavations were conducted close to the main house, where large numbers of tools would not likely be found. Iron's lack of durability may account for some of this because a majority of the tools would have been made of iron.

Transportation Equipment. No iron elements from carriages, other vehicles or from saddles were recovered. Several iron buckles from harness equipment did, however, survive. In addition, three harness ornaments and what has tentatively been identified as a terret, all of brass or a similar alloy, were found (fig. 47). The most interesting of these harness ornaments was of an alloy containing a large percentage of lead and engraved with the words C. Drayton/Charleston/S.C. Unfortunately for dating purposes, four consecutive Charles Draytons lived at the property. The form and material itself, however, would indicate that it dates from the last half of the 19th century, thus belonging to Charles Henry Drayton.

Other. Very few identifiable tool fragments were found. One small half-round rat-tail file and numerous fragments of iron that could not be positively identified, but which were classified as tools, compose the majority of labor or technological tools. Three links of a handwrought iron chain, the specific use of which could not be determined, were also recovered (fig. 48).

Subsistence Items

Procurement Equipment. The evidence for agricultural work was slender, consisting of two teeth from an iron rake, a fragment of a hoe and several pieces of iron that may be from a shovel.

There was more extensive evidence of fishing and hunting activities at the property. Lead sinkers, many made from musket balls, were found. Numerous pieces of lead shot, ranging from bird shot to buckshot, as well as larger caliber rifle balls, were found on the site (fig. 49). In addition, numerous .22 rim-fire and shotgun shell (12 gauge) cartridges were recovered, these being of 20th-century origin. About a dozen expended percussion caps were excavated, along with a few cartridges from various caliber rifles and six gun flints, two found in the driveway excavations, were recovered (fig. 50).

The amount of small shot and buckshot, along with the fact that the larger caliber shots were all round balls, seems to indicate that this material was being used for hunting game and was not the result of fighting. This supposition is further supported by the fact that there are no records of any battles being fought in the area and only tradition says that troops were ever quartered on the property. It is much more likely, since a great deal of this material was located immediately outside the house and flanker (84 of 100 pieces came from these two locations), that they were discarded as the result of dressing game or in the food refuse.

Three pieces of brass inlay, probably from the stock(s) of a gun, were found (fig. 51). Although this could have come from a weapon like the pistol for which there is evidence, these pieces have been mentioned here as more likely coming from a hunting rifle.

-Text continues on page 99

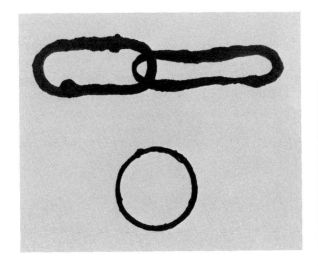

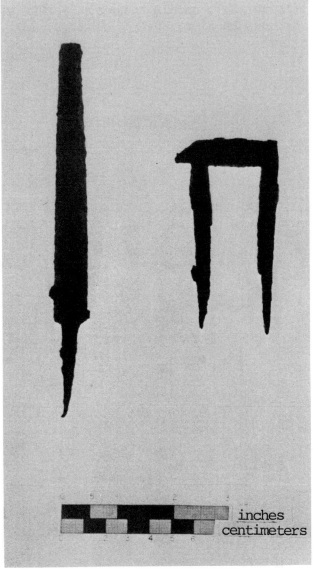

Figure 48: Miscellaneous iron objects. Upper left photo, wrought iron chain links, Unit 36B; wrought iron ring, Unit 42B. Lower left, key, Unit 38B V; key, provenience lost. Right, rat-tail file, Unit 42B/BU; rake tines, Unit 34B/BUG.

-Continued on next page

Figure 48--continued

Upper left: hinge pintle, Unit 10B/BVC; hook, Unit 11C/BDK. Lower left, unidentified tool, handle hollow to accept wooden insert (?), Unit 10B/BVH. Right,
harness buckles, Unit 22B/EZP.

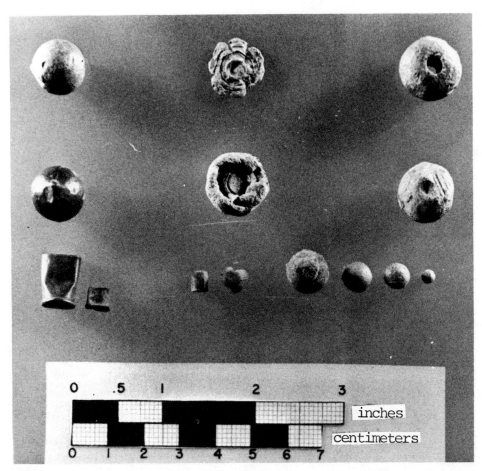

Figure 49: Munitions and gun parts. Left, in top two rows, unfired, lead round balls, Units 22B/DKV and 20E/GC; middle, top
two rows, fired lead shot, Units 38C and 20B/NV; right, top
row, lead shot drilled to be used in a sinker, Unit 38B IIIa;
right, second row, lead shot partially drilled, Unit 38B IIIa.
Bottom row, left to right: brass cartridges, Units 22B/DLC
and 33B; unfired and fired percussion caps, Units 33B and
33C/KA; lead shot from pistol ball to bird shot, Units 18B/OL,
33B Va, 35E.

98

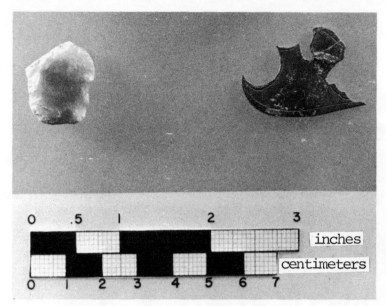

Figure 50: Left,
gray gun flint,
Unit 7B/PV;right,
brass inlay (for
gun?), Unit 38B
IIIa/VF, VG.

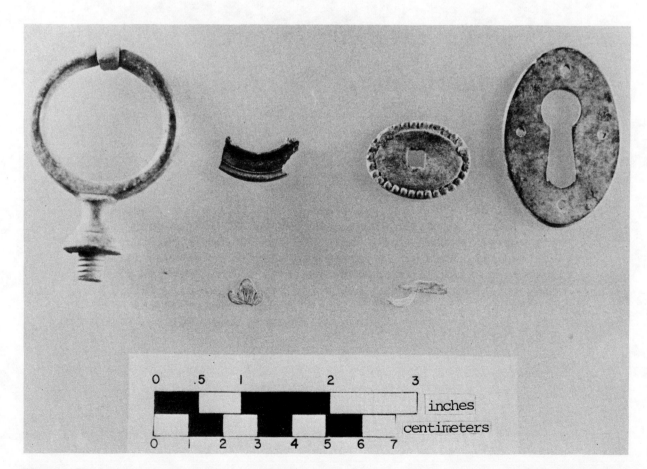

Figure 51: Miscellaneous brass. Top row, left to right: terret, Unit 42B; back
plate fragment, Unit 38B IVa, back plate, Unit 4A/ET; escutcheon, Unit 38B Va.
Bottom row, inlay, Units 38B Va, 38H.

Floral Remains. The highest concentrations of floral remains were found within the house and in Units 10 and 11. The only vegetable remains found were kernels of corn and pieces of corn cob in the cellar of the house; the balance of the floral remains consisted of nuts and fruit pits. Both peach and cherry pits were found, as well as pecan, walnut and hickory nut shells.

Faunal Remains. A detailed analysis of the bones found on this site has not been undertaken, although the bones of such domestic food animals as pigs, cows and sheep or goats were found. Also, a wide variety of nondomestic food animals including deer, squirrels, fish, birds, turtles and raccoons were excavated. Several varieties of animals that probably did not serve as a source of food, such as dogs, rodents and reptiles, were also represented on the site. A piece of worked deer antler, which might have been intended as a handle for some utensil, was also found (fig. 33).

Numerous shells were recovered, the majority of these were oyster shells. It is difficult to determine, however, the amount of oyster shell used solely for its lime content and the amount that represents food served at the Drayton table. Clam and land snail shells were also found, although snails are unlikely to have been a part of the family diet. Four fragments of egg shell were recovered from the excavation of the ground floor room.

Miscellaneous Items

Stone. Items of stone other than architectural building materials and pre-historic worked stone consisted of fossilized clams and fish vertebrae, petrified wood and bone, sharks' teeth and samples of stone not native to the area. A total of 62 fossil clams were found, more than 51 percent of which came from the mound fill. Seventy-two sharks' teeth were recovered and, sur-prisingly, the majority of them were found outside the main house, with only 11 of the balance coming from the mound fill. Cinders and marl were also sampled, the bulk of these materials being found in the driveway fill.

Wood. The majority of what was classified as identifiable wood was actually charcoal fragments large enough to be sampled. A number of other wood fragments were found but were in such poor condition that they could not be identified.

Plastic. A total of nine pieces of plastic, all from surface areas or the sod and topsoil levels, were found, including two holly leaves with berries.

INTERPRETATION

To interpret an artifact assemblage totaling more than 83,000 identified and analyzed fragments, it is necessary to return to the questions raised earlier. Although each question is dealt with separately, the answer to one may also provide an insight into another, or several other, questions.

1. Does the artifact assemblage reflect the ongoing history of the region as a whole, and of the Drayton family in particular?

Viewing the artifacts as a whole, it becomes apparent that the history of the plantation can be divided into four distinct periods, not all equally repre-sented in the archaeological record. These four periods coincide and correlate with the four major divisions in the history of the family discernible by studying the documentary record, and they reflect the fluctuations in regional fortunes.

The first and most represented period spans the years from the 1740s through the 1850s. This period includes the construction and earliest occupancy of the house during the years of greatest wealth and the flowering of the plantation system. The second period includes the Civil War and the postwar period, a time of hardship and depression. The third period covers the 1870s, when the uses of phosphate, which had long been known to exist in great abundance in the region, were fully realized. Extensive strip-mining of the property was undertaken, and the revenue this brought in saved the house and property. This brief era of prosperity lasted until 1910, when heavy taxes forced the phosphate-mining industry out of the state.

The fourth period covers the years from 1910 to 1974, when the National Trust for Historic Preservation acquired the property. During this time the Drayton family began to spend most of the year in Charleston or in Flat Rock, N.C., during the summers. By the 1960s, the house was being occupied only a few weeks of the year.

Only occasional trash heaps scattered throughout the woods attest to 20th-century activity. Those heaps nearest the house, but removed from the lawn area, do contain household debris such as enameled pots, tin cans and modern bottles. Other trash deposits further removed from the house can be associated with 20th-century activities, but not necessarily with the Drayton family. This is particularly true for the remaining evidence of moonshining and bootlegging that took place mainly during the prohibition era. The large dredge cuts created for phosphate mining often gave direct access to the river and served as excellent hiding places for stills. The remains of these stills frequently can be found associated with other modern trash.

The period of the Civil War and immediately after is notable by a lack of information on the property. It is known from family records that the house was unoccupied during the Civil War and for several years thereafter, although squatters did take up residence at the main house (Providence [R.I.] Journal, 1885) and possibly in the flankers. The abandonment of the house is best reflected in the architectural record. The slate roof evidently had fallen into disrepair, and major leaks caused the loss of all the plaster ceilings on the second floor. In addition, the squatters used the newel posts from the double staircase and the floorboards from the entrance hall for firewood. It is also possible to theorize that either neglect or squatters so badly damaged the south flanker that it was never restored. Perhaps equal damage occurred to the north flanker, but in any event it was restored. Just how much damage was done at this time to the north flanker can only be determined by a thorough investigation of that site.

There is little evidence, such as new buildings, that can be definitely ascribed to this period and very few artifacts. There is certainly no evidence of any military activity and the artifacts that can be dated to this period are few. This lack is certainly not surprising in view of the turmoil of the period, the abandonment of the house and the general poverty of the region after the war.

The phosphate mining era between the 1870s and 1910 is the next most represented period, both archaeologically and architecturally. What happened at

Drayton Hall and other plantations located in the phosphate-bearing areas is certainly not typical of the entire region or state, and a great many plantations never recovered from the Civil War and subsequent decline. Indeed, the phosphate industry is most certainly responsible for the excellent state of preservation in which the house is found today.

Phosphate produced great wealth and enabled various alterations to the house, among them replacing the slate roof with tin and the brick pediment with imbricated shingles. It seems most likely that the large quantity of nails found immediately outside the house derives from these activities. Inside the house missing plaster ceilings were replaced with bead and board ceilings, the floor was repaired and replacement newel posts were installed. A small cottage was erected just east of the north flanker, probably shortly after the earthquake of 1886 destroyed the latter. A large number of trash heaps found along the edges of the lawn and in the woods date from this period.

Major landscaping was also undertaken at this time with the building of a three-tiered mound being the most visible addition. A post-and-board fence was placed across the river side of the lawn about 50 feet from the house, and the lawn area was enclosed with wire fencing except on the east side. It is thought that the serpentine flower bed was installed at this time too.

There is ample evidence of the phosphate mining, not only in the scars on the land but also in the barn and the remains of other outbuildings erected during this period. Such debris as train rails, pickaxes and machine parts are found scattered throughout the northern portion of the property.

In the archaeological record the three foregoing periods, representing the last 110 years of the property history, are dwarfed by the quantity of material recovered from the first 120 years of occupation. More than 75 percent of the artifacts date from the first period (1740s-1850s), and the bulk of them date from between 1760 and 1830. Several interlocking factors account for the preponderance of artifacts from the first century of occupation. First, the areas excavated were largely concentrated in the immediate vicinity of the house, with only two sections dug at a distance of more than 300 yards away. Second, at that time the concept of sanitation was not particularly sophisticated. Even in the best houses trash was merely thrown out the nearest convenient opening. Third, this was the period of greatest affluence for the Drayton family and for the region as a whole, and therefore it is not surprising that there would be a greater concentration of material possessions on the property. Finally, the property was almost continuously occupied and the natural result of occupation would be more household debris. (The house was abandoned for about 10 years, however, during the Revolutionary War, a fact that does not show at all in the archaeological record.)

It is this initial period of occupation, when the house was most active, for which there is informative documentary evidence (Charles Drayton's diaries from 1789 to 1820 and his daughter Maria Henrietta's letters), which will be most intensively interpreted.

2. What do the artifacts reveal about the lifestyle of the occupants of Drayton Hall, and how do they augment the documentary record?

The original purpose of the plantation, according to family records, was to serve as a winter residence rather than a summer retreat--the opposite of that use usually ascribed to a country house. The high incidence of "fever and ague" (known today as malaria) on the low-lying plantations caused their owners to flee to Charleston each summer (Wood 1974:73) with the slaves and an overseer usually left behind. The plantation owners remained in town from about the 15th of May until the arrival of the first hard frost, usually some time in November.

Yet there is no evidence of this pattern of life in the remains from Drayton Hall. A detailed analysis of the faunal remains, particularly with an emphasis on seasonality in any of the species represented, might provide support for this lifestyle, but the artifacts do not.

Tools, other than domestic equipment, are one class of artifacts particularly notable for their lack of representation. Both agricultural and technological tools were only rarely found. This may be due in part to the poor preservation of iron in the soil around Drayton Hall, or it may be the result of a fastidiousness in the care of tools, but normal breakage and wear would be likely to increase the incidence of tools even if the latter were true. It seems rather to be a reflection of an important difference in the purpose of this plantation.

The absence of artifacts confirms an impression left by family records that Drayton Hall was never a major income-producing plantation but rather was the business and administration center for the extensive Drayton holdings. There are constant references in Drayton's diaries to the arrival of crops from other plantations for use at Drayton Hall or for shipment to Charleston for sale. Evidently these crops were being processed and stored at Drayton Hall also, for the diaries refer to such buildings as a rice mill and lodge, a cotton barn and stove, a mill and a corn barn. It is known that some limited agricultural activity was being pursued, but this was probably only enough to sustain the household. While it is granted that tools associated with these activities normally would not find their way to the main house, other plantations do present more evidence of agricultural and general labor activities than is found at Drayton Hall.

The impression that Drayton Hall was not one of the vast self-sufficient plantation complexes so common in this and other areas of the South is also highlighted by the absence of artifacts. Among all the buildings mentioned by Drayton, only the reverberatory furnace and the brick kiln indicate any home industry on the property. Further, he mentions bringing in carpenters, roofers and plumbers (lead workers) either from town or from his other plantations. This may explain the lack of technological tools, which apparently were in the possession of the workers. The proximity of the plantation to Charleston, which was easily accessible by water and later by land, encouraged this way of having work done.

With the exception of agricultural and technological tools, the artifact assemblage is large and varied, and it can be deduced that the Drayton family lived quite comfortably, if not elegantly. Neither architecture nor documents can give as clear a picture of the lifestyle of the occupants of the house as can artifacts. While Maria Henrietta Drayton might ask her father to send out some buttons from Charleston, the excavated examples can give an idea of what sort of buttons they were. When Charles Drayton grants his stepmother the use of his father's crockery, what sort of wares he was referring to can be visualized. The interplay between document and recovered artifact goes further; for example, the evidence of cutlery is extremely sparse, but the records show that an extensive amount of silver was owned (Appendix B). No glassware is mentioned in the documents, but the artifacts reflect extensive and elaborate holdings, including wine goblets, tumblers, candlesticks, bowls, plates and decanters, all of lead crystal.

The fact that there were tables and chests of drawers and other furniture can be read in the records and amplified by the artifacts. A chest of drawers and what sort of hardware it had can be visualized. It can be surmised that the Draytons had a tall case clock and perhaps a mantel clock, items not mentioned in the records. The tables it is known that they possessed can be set with different sets of dishes representing changes in ceramic fashions throughout the Drayton occupation.

By studying the architectural evidence, it can be determined that the fire-places in two second floor bedrooms were lined with delft tiles, and the recovery of tile fragments allows a determination of the design on those tiles. Further, the number and variety of patterns on the recovered tiles give evidence that perhaps more than just these two fireplaces were tiled. The large quantity of nails and window glass outside the house attests to alter-ations to the house, which can be confirmed from the architecture and explained by the documents in some instances.

Certain personal possessions and ways of life are also brought to light by looking at the artifacts. The Drayton family evidently enjoyed wine with their meals, and the men a good pipe of tobacco at the table after the ladies had withdrawn. It is not hard to imagine a young Drayton daughter flirting with a handsome visitor, coquettishly smiling behind her fan, while admiring the gentleman's handsome "diamond" (glass) sleeve buttons. He in turn compliments her on the dainty embroidery she is doing, while stooping to retrieve a thimble she has dropped. Later, while the host shows his guest a new pistol with an intriguing butt plate, he proposes a hunt for the next morning.

While this is only a hypothetical picture, it is one that can be evoked by combining the artifacts and the cultural history of an era, showing the material culture as a correlate of cultural behavior. Without the evidence of archaeology to give form and substance to the assumptions of historians and architects, the picture of the past remains two-dimensional.

3. Can a detailed analysis of the ceramics provide insight into stylistic patterns?

Because more is known today about the development and stylistic changes in ceramics throughout the 18th and early 19th centuries, a detailed study of the ceramics found at Drayton Hall can highlight any deviations from these established patterns. At the same time, questions about economic factors can be answered by a closer look at the ceramic assemblage.

The ceramics at Drayton Hall were divided on the basis of kitchen and table use, the latter category including tea as well as table services. The unusually high percentage of tablewares (68%) is in contrast to that found at other sites (Noel Hume 1962; Kelso 1974) and is certainly an indicator of the wealth of the family.

The kitchenwares follow the general patterns found throughout the colonies, with coarse earthenwares and salt-glazed stonewares being the most commonly found types. The exceptional circumstance at Drayton Hall is that the Colono-Indian wares compose almost 50 percent of the kitchen crockery, a phenomenon previously discussed.

A study of the tablewares found at Drayton Hall for the period 1740-c. 1765 reveals a notable deviation from established ceramic patterns. Until the 1740s, tin-glazed earthenware was the most popular ceramic type for table settings. This ware was rapidly replaced in popularity by the more durable white salt-glazed stonewares, which also more closely approximated the look of porcelain. Finally, during the 1760s the newly developed creamware became the most widely used ceramic type. Porcelain was used throughout this time, but mainly as a tea ware.

It would be reasonable to assume that the Drayton family would follow this general pattern. At the time they took up residence at Drayton Hall, about 1742, they would have had only a few older plates of tin-glazed earthenware, a set of white salt-glazed stoneware plates and a porcelain tea set. Yet there was a surprising lack of white salt-glazed stoneware table service pieces recovered from the Drayton Hall investigations. While other sites have a high incidence of plates of this ware, there were fewer than a dozen found in the excavations at Drayton Hall. A large number of white salt-glazed sherds from chamber pots were found (fig. 52), along with fragments from tea wares, mugs and the relief-decorated teapot.

This poses the question of what the family was using for plates before the 1760s. An analysis of the porcelain vessel forms provides the answer. The Drayton family had at least two dinner services of Chinese export porcelain. One set was of plain blue and white decorated ware. There was also at least one service of overglaze decorated porcelain dinner plates. In one case it was possible to identify fragments from eight or nine separate plates of one particular overglaze design (fig. 53). The discovery of this number of plates from one set is most important, indicating that it was either broken in one large accident or was frequently used and pieces broken over a period of years. Two fragments, representing two plates, were recovered from the occupation level around the south flanker; the balance of the sherds were recovered in the occupational debris outside the side door of the main house. This makes it possible to hypothesize that a number of plates were broken at one time and swept out the door. The overglaze decorated porcelain sherds outnumbered the blue and white decorated ones (plain sherds were not included in either category).

As mentioned earlier, the presence of porcelain on a site is one indicator of wealth, particularly during the 18th century (Stone 1970:88). During the 19th century when porcelain was directly imported into the United States in enormous quantities, the ware was inexpensive and the quality deteriorated sharply. The recovery of porcelain, even overglaze decorated wares, from 19th-century sites is not a totally reliable indicator of a family's financial status, although it remains a positive indicator to some degree (Herman, Sands and Schecter 1975:66). The trend from fine early porcelain to later low quality porcelain can be observed at Drayton Hall quite clearly, and it is noteworthy that porcelain constitutes a decreasing proportion of the ceramic assemblage through time.

Figure 52: White salt-glazed stoneware chamber pot (7-3/16" across top), Unit 38B IIIa, 38B Va, 38H.

Figure 53: Sherds of overglaze enameled Chinese export porcelain; from two of eight plates with identical pattern (all, scale 1:4). Side from Unit 38L/GS. Bottom left, from Unit 34B, right, Unit 38B Va.

Another unusual factor about the Drayton porcelains is the occurrence of atypical wares. There are several pieces of unusual porcelain that are either provincial Chinese or Japanese and a tea cup, thought to be a rarely found Chinese soft paste porcelain. The recovery of several sherds of English porcelain, representing at least five vessels, further demonstrates the range and quality of the porcelain assemblage. During the 18th century, English (and continental) porcelains could not compete with the less expensive Chinese import wares, despite the tremendous distance the Chinese wares had to be shipped. Thus European porcelains appear infrequently on colonial sites, usually only in the wealthiest of 18th-century residences.

One type of pottery that is unaccountably scarce is the Whieldon-Wedgwood wares: tortoiseshell, clouded, and fruit and vegetable motif types. These were transitional between the salt-glazed stonewares and the creamwares and may not have been used because the porcelain was still popular or simply as a matter of taste. The family may not have liked this style of ware. It was very popular for a brief period, but there was very little of it found at Drayton Hall.

Creamware was first manufactured and perfected in England about 1762 (Noel Hume, 1974:125) and rapidly replaced the white salt-glazed stonewares as the most popular ceramic type. Certainly at Drayton Hall this is the case, and the creamwares evidently also replaced the porcelains as the most favored table service. This could be explained by the fact that creamware was new and fashionable or possibly it was because the overglaze decorated porcelain plates had deteriorated by this time; the overglaze decoration tended to wear off with use. Porcelain was still being used for tea service, although the variety of teapots found on the site steadily increased. By the close of the 18th century the Draytons had or once had in use not only porcelain but also white salt-glazed stoneware, jasper-type ware, "black basalte," red dry-bodied stoneware, "jackfield" ware, creamware and probably pearlware teapots.

Creamware was the most common ceramic type found at Drayton Hall, with the largest number of plates, platters and soup plates being of this ware. Judging from the rim fragments, there must have been a large set of old feather-edge style tablewares and perhaps a smaller or breakfast set of the royal pattern. The beaded edges all derived from tea wares. No diamond-pattern rim sherds were found, in contrast to the findings on other sites (South 1974; Kelso 1974; Fairbanks, personal communication).

Immediately after and perhaps during the Revolutionary War, Rouen faience, a type of ware from France, became very popular in the United States. This was a poorly made ware, dark brown lead-glazed on the exterior, white tin-glazed on the interior. It usually had a brown band of decoration around the interior rim and sometimes a medallion-like design at the center. This ware was commonly found on post-Revolution sites (Noel Hume 1969:599-61) and its total absence at Drayton Hall is noteworthy. It was certainly still being imported into Charleston (Prime 1969:146) but the Draytons obviously made little or no use of it. This again might be a matter of the Drayton's taste in ceramics. They evidently liked to keep up with the latest and best in ceramics, which the Rouen faience certainly was not. That large amounts of it were found at Fort Moultrie (South 1974), where it would have been used by poorly paid soldiers, indicates that it was a poorer class of ware and was perhaps absent by choice of the family.

During the last quarter of the 18th century, pearlware was developed in England. This new ware was extremely white and well adapted to various decorative techniques, particularly transfer printing. Transfer printing had been tried on creamware, but with the exception of black over-the-glaze printing, was not well suited to this ware. It was shortly after the development of pearlware, with its blue cast due to the inclusion of cobalt in the glaze, that blue under-glaze transfer printing was tried and became tremendously successful. In fact, blue transfer-printed wares rapidly replaced all other wares in popularity, a fashion that lasted well into the 19th century. Transfer printing was such a practical, low-cost method of embellishment that it also appeared on the newly developed whitewares in the 19th century and is still in use today. In the late 1820s other colors besides blue were introduced.

Before the development of blue transfer-printed wares, pearlware was most commonly decorated with a molded, shell-edge design, which was then painted green, blue or, less frequently, red or yellow. The Drayton family quickly adopted these wares and evidently had a set of both green and blue-edged plates. These, though, were certainly rapidly replaced by the transfer-printed pearlwares, which included not only plates but also teapots, cups, saucers and jars. Of all the wares found at Drayton Hall, the blue transfer-printed pearlwares showed the greatest variety in vessel form. Both the well-known "willow" pattern, and a variety of other scenic patterns are found among the designs.

Whitewares became popular during the second quarter of the 19th century, although Mason patented his "Ironstone China" in 1813. Only a small amount of whiteware was found in the excavations, but this may be due more to changing trash disposal habits than to that ware's lack of popularity.

Overall, the Drayton family appears to have kept current with the latest in ceramic styles and, in one case, favored a more costly ware over an equally available but less costly one. The high incidence of overglaze enameled porcelains is remarkable, as is the consistent quality of these wares. In use at a time when white salt-glazed stonewares were quite popular, it shows the ability of the family to afford the best for their table. At the same time, the family was not extravagant and made use of the locally (if not home) made, inexpensive Colono-Indian wares for their kitchen. Long thought to have been the pottery of slaves or poor laborers, it is evident, at least in Charleston, that this pottery was extremely practical, readily available and widely used.

4. Can the wealth of the family, or other economic factors, be determined from the artifacts?

Earlier in this discussion of ceramics, it was pointed out that certain trends in the ceramic consumption pattern of a family can indicate wealth, particularly for the 18th century. At Cannon's Point, a 19th-century plantation in Georgia, an attempt was made to determine whether a distinction could be made between the residential sites of a planter, an overseer and the slaves on the basis of the recovered artifacts (Otto 1975). It was noted that there was a difference both in type of ceramics present and in variety of vessel forms among these three sites; in particular, it was observed that less than 1 percent of the planter's ceramic assemblage consisted of annular pearlwares, while almost 12 percent of the ceramics were transfer-printed wares (Otto 1975:220). In comparison, at Drayton Hall the annular wares represented

more than 4 percent of all the ceramics, while the transfer-printed wares
constituted 7.6 percent of all the ceramics. Otto postulates that a high
incidence of transfer-printed ware is indicative of wealth, and while it
outnumbers the annular ware at Drayton Hall, it is not as common as it was
at Cannon's Point. The criterion of vessel form, however, does seem more valid
than sherd count and the fact that almost all the banded wares were bowls, a
form most likely to be used in the kitchen, would indicate a difference in
the status of the wares. The transfer-printed wares were tablewares, plates
and tea cups and other vessels that would appear "above stairs" and not
remain in the kitchen.

It is not possible to make a direct comparison at Drayton Hall, since no slave
or overseer sites were excavated. It is possible, however, to hypothesize on
the basis of these observations that banded pearlware bowls might well be
found in large quantities at the main house along with even larger quantities
and varieties of transfer-printed pearlwares. Thus, a larger than 1 percent
occurrence of annular wares at a known planter's house is not necessarily a
negative indicator of wealth but more likely represents the division between
wares that stay in the kitchen and those that appear on the table. In support
of this idea, it should be noted that there is no indication of declining
family wealth, either in the documents or in the total artifact assemblage.
This seems, rather, to be a matter of economy where it does not show.
Certainly they were using the least expensive of wares, the Colono-Indian
ceramics, at the same time as the most costly porcelains were in use.

In 1974, George Miller, then laboratory curator for the St. Mary's City (Md.)
Commission, analyzed the ceramics from a tenant farmer's house in St. Mary's
County. He found a large number of green and blue shell-edge pearlware
fragments, all of the same basic pattern but different styles and quality of
execution. He hypothesized that this poor farmer was buying his ceramics a
piece at a time and was unable to exactly match the patterns from purchase
to purchase (Miller 1974).

Analyzing both the creamware (old feather edge) and the pearlware (shell edge)
fragments from Drayton Hall, it became obvious that even a wealthy family like
the Draytons was unable to consistently match patterns. Of the 55 old feather
edge creamware fragments found, enough were exact matches but from differing
vessels to indicate that a set had once been purchased, but more than 50 percent of the fragments were of the same, but nonmatching, pattern. This was
also true for the shell-edge pearlwares, with even less incidence of identical patterns. It seems then that difficulty in matching patterns is not
necessarily a product of poverty but rather is due to the large number of
English manufacturers all producing the same patterns, each one differing
slightly, or to a single manufacturer using different mold makers. The one
indication of wealth that might be established by a study of rim patterns is
the initial purchase of a set, with differing replacement pieces, rather than
the presence of an array of single mismatched pieces.

The amount of lead crystal table glass found on the site is another indicator
of the general well-being of the family. It was expensive, and to find the
majority of glassware, as well as several ornamental pieces, of this type
would indicate wealth.

Aside from these observations, the fact that the Draytons could afford to maintain a nonincome-producing plantation as well as a town house, not to mention their other vast holdings, indicates wealth, and the sheer size of the artifact assemblage is a manifestation of this status. More than 10,000 ceramic sherds, more than 900 pipe fragments, more than 4,000 sherds of bottle glass and more than 700 of table glass, as well as almost 100 buttons were recovered. The variety and quantity of these artifacts attest to the wealth of the family.

5. What patterns of property and structure usage can be determined from a distributional analysis of the artifacts? Do patterns of garbage disposal follow those discovered on other Anglo-American sites? Are particular travel patterns discernible and can architectural details be determined from such an analysis?

This group of questions is important to any analysis of a site and its artifacts because they ask more of the data than merely what was present. They assume that there are patterns to human behavior and that the artifacts, be they a rich family's or a poor family's, did not randomly come to be distributed about a site. Artifacts are present because of people's deliberate activity (with the exception of accidental losses, such as a coin falling from a pocket).

A detailed distributional analysis of the artifacts found in the excavation of the south flanker has previously been discussed. The fact that such an analysis can help determine the placement of architectural features, such as doors and windows, and that a pattern of destruction could be hypothesized should point to the utility of this type of analysis.

Only limited travel patterns were discernible by a distributional analysis, but this was more likely the result of the nature of the excavations rather than a fault of the data. It was obvious that as one moved from the house toward the flanker, the occurrence of artifacts decreased and then rose again, with the lowest incidence occurring about midway between the two buildings. Also, the density of artifacts immediately in front of the side door of the main house was the lowest, certainly due to material being tossed to either side of the door and to foot traffic knocking artifacts to the side.

The garbage disposal pattern is similar to that found on other Anglo-American sites, with holes and, later, ditches being used to contain the trash when convenient, with the back yard receiving its share of debris. The drive in particular is a good example of this method, where household debris was used to fill in potholes and level the driveway. It is of interest to note that the later the date of the garbage, the farther it is found from a building. The homes of the poorer class and slaves, where more sophisticated concepts of sanitation did not occur until later, might prove to be an exception to this pattern.

Even in the case of early deposits, the organic debris is more likely to be found at a greater distance from the main house. While ceramic, glass and other nonorganic debris was common around the house itself, the number of bones found outside the south flanker was 6.5 times greater than around the house. In fact, this was the largest concentration of bone found, thus giving credence to the theory that at least the room with the fireplace was used for kitchen activities. On the other hand, the incidence of porcelain is 4.4 times greater around the main house than outside the flanker.

Other anomalies in distribution, such as the fact that the majority of furniture hardware was found outside the flanker, lead to interesting theories. On the basis of the analysis of artifact distribution and the observation of architectural detail it was hypothesized that the south flanker was intentionally razed. Also, based on a chronological analysis of the artifacts, particularly the ceramics, it was noted that the average date for the ceramics was rather early for a building that probably stood for at least 150 years. It was thus theorized, with the help of some early photographs, that the building changed function, probably after the War between the States, and was used for storage. Almost six times more pieces of furniture hardware were found around the flanker than around the main house, making it tempting to imagine that outdated, unwanted pieces of furniture were being stored in the flanker and that they subsequently were destroyed or allowed to deteriorate and were discarded when the building was razed. This becomes even more likely when it is noted that the majority of this hardware dates from the second half of the 18th century. Such observations can bolster or refute hypotheses and go beyond the observations of architecture and the documents to determine function or alteration of function. It is a very important use for the artifactual data.

As has been demonstrated throughout the Drayton Hall archaeological project, the archaeological records constantly and productively interact with the work of the architectural historian and the historical architect. A question asked by one may be answered by the other, or assumptions held by one may be confirmed or denied by data discovered by the other. For a historical site, this constant interaction on the part of three disciplines that frequently operate separately can be of great value to one attempting to understand the history of a property and interpret that history to the public.

In addition to this important function of the archaeological excavations, there is the more general purpose of adding to the knowledge of the past, and in the case of Drayton Hall to the understanding of patterns of life in low country South Carolina. Further, questions and techniques posed by archaeologists can be addressed or applied in the course of the excavations. New ways of looking at the remains of the past can be proposed and tested.

At the conclusion of the Drayton Hall archaeological project, plans to stabilize and restore the foundations of the south flanker and the connecting wall between the house and that flanker were being implemented. At the outset of the project it was determined that the flanker would not be restored in its entirety, but that its basic outlines, including the chimney and stairway foundations, would be retained just above the present grade. The same was planned for the connecting wall; however, serious deterioration of this wall had been caused by tree root growth and it was necessary to reconstruct portions of the wall. The purpose of this reconstruction was to give a sense of scale and a feeling for the sophisticated architectural plan conceived by the builder of Drayton Hall. This work was recently completed.

Although much work has been done on fort sites in the Southeast and a Charleston town house (the Heyward-Washington House) is currently being excavated, there have been no intensive studies of South Carolina plantation sites. It would be of great value, therefore, to carry out further study of this plantation.

Although a number of important areas were excavated in the course of the preliminary investigations, several critical areas remain to be explored. Archaeological investigations should be resumed in the near future and should include exploration of the north flanker (for comparison with the south flanker), the 18th-century orangery and the area of the suspected slave avenue. Work on these areas certainly should be incorporated into the Drayton Hall master plan. Further, thorough investigation of any area that would be altered by construction and its attendant disturbances should be mandatory. The quantities of information and artifacts found on the property, particularly in the lawn area, reemphasize the need for extreme caution before breaking ground.

This abbreviated Drayton family tree emphasizes the branch that owned Drayton Hall. Owners names are in capitals.

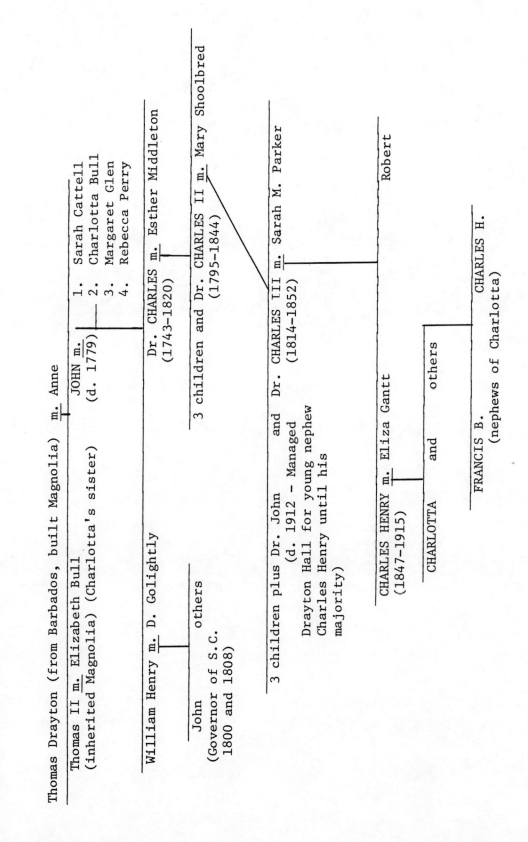

Thomas Drayton (from Barbados, built Magnolia) m. Anne

Thomas II m. Elizabeth Bull
(inherited Magnolia) (Charlotta's sister)

JOHN m.
(d. 1779)

1. Sarah Cattell
2. Charlotta Bull
3. Margaret Glen
4. Rebecca Perry

Dr. CHARLES m. Esther Middleton
(1743–1820)

3 children and Dr. CHARLES II m. Mary Shoolbred
(1795–1844)

William Henry m. D. Golightly

John   others
(Governor of S.C.
1800 and 1808)

3 children plus Dr. John and Dr. CHARLES III m. Sarah M. Parker
(d. 1912 – Managed   (1814–1852)
Drayton Hall for young nephew
Charles Henry until his
majority)

Robert

CHARLES HENRY m. Eliza Gantt
(1847–1915)

CHARLOTTA   and   others

FRANCIS B.   CHARLES H.
(nephews of Charlotta)

This appendix lists examples of the types of household goods owned by members of the Drayton family. There are no direct records of ownership, the closest being the list of household goods that Charles Drayton turned over to his step-mother for use during her lifetime. From these records it can be seen that the archaeologist only recovers a small portion of those goods that a low country plantation owner would have, but that which is recovered amplifies and defines certain classes of items such as "Tea Cups + Saucers" mentioned in the records.

From Miscellaneous Records and Bills of Sale, Volume FF, pp. 433-34, 26 August 1745: Bill of Sale of Household Goods, "from John Drayton of the Parish of St. Andrew in the County of Berkley to Thomas Ladson For the sum of 220 pounds 19 shillings of good + lawfull money of the province"- sold -

> ...Two feather beds and Bedsteads Four blanketts two Rugs two p^{rs} of Sheets/ two Bolsters four pillows one Cannue + tackling one bay riding horse branded E two/ mare Colts one horfe branded JD two heifers Two Steirs mark'd with an under keel/ on the right Ear and upper keel on the left one large deel cheft four pine Boxes nine/ black Chairs one square Cyprefs Table one Ceader ditto half a doz Tea Cups + Saucers/ four Iron potts two tea kettles two p^{r} of tongs on[e] fire Shovell one p^{r} of Doggs one Cote and/ Bed one dozen pewter plates three dishes fiftein pewter Spoons of which Particulars I/ have given him the said Thomas Ladfon an Inventory....

From Miscellaneous Records and Bills of Sale, Volume YY, pp. 477-79, 10 September 1783, Charles Drayton turned over certain household items to his father's widow Rebecca. These items are to be his on Rebecca's death but he turned them over to her for her use for the sum of 5 pounds:

> ...two Dozen large knives + forks/ one Dozen Desert Do [ditto] one dozen table Spoons, one dozen desert do/ one Soup Spoon, one pair of butter boats, one pair of Salt Sellers/ one set of Castors, two pair of Candlesticks, one Coffee Pot, two/ pair of waiters, one bread basket, Six tea Spoons, one cream pot/ a childs pap boat - all the above are of Silver. Nine Mahogany/ tables, three sets of Chests of Drawer's, one library table, three/ sets of bed steads, one Chest, one large trunck, one Cribb + Cradle./ two floor Carpets, two Marble Slabbs, and Stands, three--/ Chimney grates and backs, two Sopha's, four armed Chairs/ one large Gilt framed Looking Glafs, two small drefsing--/ Glafses - the Crockery ware, bed furniture and table Linnen -/ Marble Mortar - and a Cow.

116

From Inventories, Wills and Miscellaneous Papers, Volume 85B (1758-61), pp. 984-92, 4 April 1761: Inventory of household possessions of Thomas Drayton (II), brother of John Drayton.

Item	Pounds	Shillings	Pence
1 Large Clock	60		
Mahogany Desk	35		
1 p^r Gilt Sconces	45		
1 Large Japan'd do [ditto]	45		
1 Couch 1 doz Chairs 1 Easy d^o Mahog.	150		
2 Mahogany Tables	14		
1 Glass Scruitor	150		
1 Mahogany Cupboard	35		
1 d^o Tea Table	15		
1 Large Cedar Table	5		
1 Mahog^y Side Board d^o	5		
12 Glaz'd Prints	18		
Books	60		
6 Mahog^y Chairs 1 Elbow d^o	23		
2 Japand Cup boards	2		
1 Mahog^y Bed stead Mattrass & furnit^r	200		
1 Mahogany Chest of Drawers	45		
1 Dressing Table and Glass	7		
De Brahams map	5		
1 Wainscot Bed stead Bed & furnit^e	45		
1 Small Mattrass, Pillow & Bolster	15		
8 p^s & 1/2 Negro Cloth	360		
1 Small Cedar Table	1		
1 Large hair Trunk	5		
1 Wainscot Bed stead Bed & Mattress	20		
1 Dressing Table and Glass	4		
5 old Trunks	7		
2 Bridles, 10 Girths 7 Dog Couples 2 Portmanteau Straps all new	5		
Gun Powder and Shott	20		
1 Barrel of old Iron and Lead	2	10	
1 Mahogany Chest of Drawers	10		
1 Small Walnut Table	3		
1 Small Mattrass, Pillows & Pavilion	12		
1 Screen	25		
Tin Ware, new	7		
Pewter Plate and Dishes	70		
2 new Bed Ticks Pillows & Bolster	30		
1 Large Portmanteau	5		
2 New Pavilions	25		
1 Marble Mortar and Pestle	5		
Basons and Stone Ware	1	10	
2 Glass Lanthorns	5		
1 Brass & 1 Iron Appartus for mak^g Lines	12		
1 Chocolate 1 Coffee pott 1 Brass Cock and Ladle	1	10	
One Warming pan	2	10	
1 Saddle and Blue Furniture	18		
1 Cloths Press	5		
2 Bed Quilts & some Remnants	20		

Item	Pounds	Shillings	Pence
1 Copper Still	80		
1 Poplar Bed stead		10	
1 Mahag^y d^o Bed furniture & Window Curtains	75		
1 Small Wainscot d^o with furniture	40		
1 Mahogany Desk	15		
1 d^o Dressing Glass	6		
1 pr Brass and Irons	10		
1 Large p^r d^o	12		
1 Iron d^o Brass heads	12		
China Ware	125		
Stone d^o	35		
Glass d^o	35		
1 Dutch Tea Kettle & Lamp	3	10	
2 Razor Cases with Razors Box and Brush	4		
1 Set of Castors	10		
2 p^r Brass Large Candlesticks	14		
1 Lignum Vitae 1 Copper Mortar & Pestles	5		
1 Brass Hearth	10		
1 Tankard 1 Sauce Boat 1 Porringer 1 Salver 11 Table Spoons 1 Soup d^o 10 Tea d^o 1 Strainer 1 Tea tong 4 Salts 1 Pint Mug 1 Punch Ladle all Silver at thirty five Shillings p^r Ounce			
1 Brass mounted Gun	40		
1 d^o twenty five pounds	5		
1 Silver mounted d^o	10		
1 d^o Thirty pounds	30		
1 Brass mounted d^o	4		
1 p^r Silver mounted pistols	70		
2 d^o Swords	60		
1 Black d^o 1 Cuttoe	1		
1 Large & other Trunks	3	10	
1 Small Still	20		
1 Large Case of Bottles	9		
old Iron	15		
Plantation Tools	35		
Juggs	7	10	
1 Case of Bottles	7		
2 half Barrels of Nails	80		
1 Box of Scythe Stones	0	15	
1 Wolf Trap	7		
3 Copper Tea kettles 1 Chafing dish	6		
1 Coffee Mill	2		
1 Plate Warmer	1	10	
Shoemakers Tools	2		
1 Ox Cart and Chains	35		
Sixty one Sheep @ 45/p^r h^d			
20 Hogs at 20/p^r head			
Forty two horses @ £5 d^o			
four hunting d^o @ thirty pounds			
Thirteen Oxen at thirteen pounds p^r h^d			
Sixty eight Cows and Calves at five pounds p^r head			
1 Large Copper Kettle	15		

APPENDIX C: DIMENSIONAL AND PROVENIENCE CONTROL DATA

Each excavation unit opened during the course of the Drayton Hall project was assigned a provenience control number (unit number) and strata and features within each unit were assigned a letter in addition to the number. A provenience card was kept on each unit and level. Such data as the horizontal location, the opening and closing elevation, a sketch of each level or feature, a description of the tools used in excavating, a stratum description and a brief list of recovered artifacts were recorded. In some cases, a level or feature assigned a control number and letter was subsequently voided and incorporated with another feature or level. The letters L or J and O were always omitted when assigning a provenience number and letter to avoid any confusion.

In addition, profile and plan drawings, a survey log and a day book were kept as a means of data storage and control. Black and white and/or color photographs were taken of many units and a photo log was kept. This log records the orientation, subject, date, film type and any special lenses or filters used, negative number and file number of each photograph taken.

Following is a brief description of each unit excavated, with notations on the existence of drawings and/or photographs: An * designates photograph; + profile drawings; and # plan view. The location of each unit may be determined by referring to the site plan (fig. 2). Dimensions given are for the overall size of units or its A level.

PROVENIENCE NUMBER AND LOCATION	UNIT SIZE	DESCRIPTION AND WORK DONE
*1A Driveway	5' x 6.5'	Below a layer of leaf mold, removed a thin level of dark brown sandy loam mottled with 10% gray brown sandy loam and 10% tan yellow sandy loam.
+1B		A level of brown sandy loam mottled with 10% tan yellow sandy loam and 10% tan gray sandy loam, mixed with brick and plaster crumbs.
+1C		Removed an oblong intrusion of brown sandy loam mixed with brick crumbs. This appeared to be a pothole, about 2' x 1', which had been filled in with brick and cinders.
+1D		A large area of gray brown sandy loam mixed with ashes and mottled with 10% tan yellow sandy loam. This level, along with 1A and 1B, contained modern artifacts and appears to be the result of constant filling of the driveway with cinders, ashes, brick and assorted trash.
+1E		Removed a linear intrusion of reddish brown loam mixed with small brick crumbs. The intrusion was 0.7' wide and ran parallel to the driveway, appearing to be a rut that had silted over.
+1F		A level of tan brown sandy loam and tan yellow sandy loam, about equally mixed, was explored and as expected contained no artifacts. This soil type is the typical subsoil, generally sterile except for fossils, over the western two thirds of the property, as determined from the test holes.
+2A Driveway +3A	5' x 10' 5' x 10'	Sod and topsoil, consisting of dark brown sandy loam mixed with brick fragments and containing numerous modern artifacts.
+2B		Removed a level of dark brown sandy loam mixed with brick fragments and crumbs. This was evidently a fill covering the driveway after it had fallen into disuse.

NOTE: * designates photograph; + profile drawing; and # plan view.

PROVENIENCE NUMBER AND LOCATION	UNIT SIZE	DESCRIPTION AND WORK DONE
*2C		A shallow, semicircular intrusion of dark brown sandy loam heavily flecked with brick crumbs was removed. It contained a fragment of tin can, several restorable sherds of blue willow transfer-print on whiteware and a padlock. It appeared to be a pothole filled in with garbage.
*#2D *#2E		Removed a narrow linear intrusion of dark brown sandy loam mottled with 20% tan brown loamy sand and mixed with a heavy concentration of brickbats and crumbs. These two features represent filled ruts in the driveway. Along with the heavy concentration of brick, the ruts contained glass, nails, bone, charcoal and some ceramics.
+*#2F		This feature of dark brown sandy loam mottled with 10% tan-brown sandy loam and occasional brick, brick fragments and crumbs separated the ruts (2D and 2E) in the driveway and was distinguished by a much lighter concentration of brick but a substantially heavier concentration of household debris.
*#2G		A narrow linear intrusion of dark brown sandy loam mixed with occasional marl fragments and brick crumbs was removed and was apparently a mixture of fills from driveway rut 2E and the marl-filled ditch 3C. Beyond brick crumbs and a brickbat, the only artifact recovered was a small piece of mortar.
*#2H *#2I		Below 2F, two small linear intrusions of gray-white sand, containing no artifacts, were removed. These were apparently caused by water running down the drive, depositing the sand. Both were very shallow, less than .1' deep.
*#2K		Along the southern edge of Unit 2 a level of dark brown sandy loam mottled with 5% gray-brown sand was removed. This area contained very few artifacts and went down to the subsoil level. It was determined that this represented the old topsoil in this area.

PROVENIENCE NUMBER AND LOCATION	UNIT SIZE	DESCRIPTION AND WORK DONE
*+#2L		Removed a large oblong intrusion of very dark brown sandy loam mixed with occasional brick crumbs down to subsoil. It contained a kaolin pipe stem, several burned brick fragments and eight pieces of prehistoric Indian pottery. From the irregularity of the feature, it was determined that it was a root mold.
*#2M		Removed a very irregular intrusion of brown sandy loam mottled with tan-brown clayey loam, containing only two artifacts. This was extremely thin and evidently the remnants of the driveway fill.
2N	5' x 10'	Sod and topsoil, consisting of dark brown sandy loam mixed with brick fragments. This was an extension of Unit 2, opened to expose the top of the driveway.
*#3B Driveway		This circular intrusion of dark brown sandy loam contained two pieces of prehistoric Indian pottery and a small brick fragment. It was 1' x 1.5' in plan and .65' deep. Not a root mold, it was either a posthole or perhaps some sort of Indian feature.
*+#3C		Removed a level of very dark brown sandy loam mottled with 50% tan-yellow clayey loam and tan brown loamy sand mixed with numerous marl chunks in the southern quarter of Unit 3. This was evidently a ditch cut along the northern side of the driveway and filled with subsoil to aid drainage. A similar ditch was not found on the southern side of the drive, probably because the ground slopes away from the drive toward the pond on that side. Only fossil artifacts were recovered.
*+#3D 3E (voided; incorporated with 3D)		This feature (and the voided feature 3E) of tan-brown sandy loam mottled with 10% yellow sand and 10% gray brown loamy sand was a large root mold containing no artifacts.

NOTE: * designates photograph; + profile drawing; and # plan view.

122

PROVENIENCE NUMBER AND LOCATION	UNIT SIZE	DESCRIPTION AND WORK DONE
*#3F 3G (voided; incorporated with 3F)		This feature was also a root mold, consisting of tan brown sandy loam mottled with 10% yellow sand and 10% gray brown loamy sand. Only two very small fragments of prehistoric pottery were found. Feature 3F when combined with the voided 3G, ran into feature 3D(3E) to form one very large tree root mold.
3H		Below the marl-filled ditch (3C) removed a linear intrusion of dark brown sandy loam mottled with 15% tan-yellow sandy loam down to subsoil. This area was a continuation of the driveway ditch, but contained no marl. One machine cut nail and several brick and bone fragments were the only artifacts recovered.
*#3I *#3K *#3L		These three features were part of the large root mold 3D and 3F and consisted of medium brown sandy loam mottled with 10% tan brown sandy loam and 10% yellow brown sandy loam. Only a few pieces of prehistoric pottery were found.
#4A Ground floor NE room	7.23' x 10'	Removed a very thin layer of dark brown sandy loam mixed with organic debris, window glass, plaster and brick flecks. This was the dust and loose debris on the ground-level floor caused by usage.
8A	10' x 10'	
#4B		Removed a shelf of heavy plaster debris mixed with dark brown sandy loam, mottled with brick dust and charcoal flecks. The plaster shelf was evidently a mound swept together after the plaster ceiling had collapsed or been removed and contained fragments of glass, ceramics, nails, pipe stem and bone.
#+4C		Removed a level of very dark brown sandy loam, very loosely compacted and mixed with plaster and brick dust. This was an area along the interior walls that had been disturbed during the early 1950s when extensive termite extermination was carried out.

PROVENIENCE NUMBER AND LOCATION	UNIT SIZE	DESCRIPTION AND WORK DONE
*4D		A large number of wandering irregular intrusions of loosely compacted grayish brown sandy loam with plaster crumbs were excavated. These were rodent burrows, containing numerous bones, organic remains and some ceramics and glass. On completion of this area, more than half of the excavation unit was taken up by the burrows.
4E		A mixed fill of light grayish brown sandy loam mottled with numerous plaster flecks and brickbats was removed from the area immediately adjacent to the termite trench (4C) along the western wall. It contained numerous artifacts including tin-glazed earthenware and whiteware, nails, glass, white clay pipe stems, and bone. Three whole bricks and several brickbats were located in this area, aligned in such a manner that it is possible these are remnants of a brick floor. The quantities of artifacts in this area indicated that perhaps when the floor was removed trash was dumped in this room.
4F		Very dark brown sandy loam, tightly packed, was removed from this area, which had been badly eroded by the rodent action. This area apparently either underlay the brick floor or was the original hard-packed earth floor. The former is more likely, a hypothesis supported by the fact that only seven artifacts were found.
+4G		This area, the builder's trench, consisted of dark brown sandy loam mottled with 10% yellow clay. Only the bottom 0.1-0.2' remained and the bottom of the trench, which was subsoil, contained scattered brick rubble. No artifacts were recovered from this portion of the trench.
+5A Driveway & Mound	5' x 10'	Sod and topsoil consisting of dark brown sandy loam was removed from these areas. A variety of artifacts, ranging from whiteware to modern green bottle glass to half of a horseshoe were found at this level.
+6A	5' x 10'	
+7A	5' x 10'	
+9A	5' x 10'	

NOTE: * designates photograph; + profile drawing; and # plan view.

124

PROVENIENCE NUMBER AND LOCATION	UNIT SIZE	DESCRIPTION AND WORK DONE
+5B 5G		Covering the western two thirds of this unit beneath the sod and topsoil a level of very dark gray-brown clayey loam mottled with 10% light gray clay was removed. It contained one creamware sherd, brick fragments, fossils and bone and was the first layer of clay used to construct the mound.
+5C		In the western third of this unit, below the sod and topsoil, a level of dark brown sandy loam mottled with 10% tan yellow loamy sand was removed. This was a portion of the mound fill and contained very few artifacts.
+5D 5H		Below the mound fill 5B and 5C removed a four-foot-wide level of very dark gray brown clayey loam mottled with 50% light gray clay. This area was apparently a portion of the circular return, which was the terminus of the driveway. Almost no artifacts were recovered, indicating that this portion of the drive either suffered less from travel or was better cared for, the latter being quite possible judging from the large quantities of clay in this area.
+5E		Below 5C removed a level of very dark brown clayey loam with occasional brick crumbs and mortar flecks. Only a few artifacts were found in this area, which was apparently part of the old topsoil.
5F	5' x 9.5'	Sod and topsoil consisting of dark brown sandy loam was removed from this unit, which was an extension of the original 5' x 10' Unit 5 an additional 5' northward. Only three artifacts were found.
#+5I		Below 5H removed a lense of light brown sandy loam mixed with many cinders and pebbles. This was a very small area and probably represents a fill used in the driveway.

PROVENIENCE NUMBER AND LOCATION	UNIT SIZE	DESCRIPTION AND WORK DONE

+6B — Beneath the sod and topsoil a level of dark brown sandy loam with pockets of fine gravel mixed with dark brown sandy loam was removed. On inspection of the profile it could be seen that these areas of gravel ran in a continuous line beginning approximately 7' from the driveway bed, or, in other words, beginning where disturbance for the mound construction ended. Charles Drayton makes reference to a graveled court, and it is thought that this gravel may represent that court, along with the gravel found in 7B.

*+6C — Below 6B removed a circular intrusion of yellow brown sandy clay mottled with 10% dark brown sandy loam and 10% light tan brown sandy clay. This, along with feature 6D, was a posthole and mold, probably dating from the period when this area was fenced for a rose garden.

*+6D — Removed a square intrusion of very dark gray brown sandy loam mottled with 10% yellow sandy clay. This post mold contained no artifacts.

6E — Below 6B removed a level of dark brown sandy loam mottled with 20% tan brown sandy loam down to subsoil. This area, which contained only a few artifacts represents the old topsoil.

+7B — Below the sod and topsoil, removed a level of dark brown sandy loam mottled with 10% tan brown sandy loam and mixed with brick crumbs. This level contained some of the gravel found in 6B, but it only extended about 1' into the western end of the unit. The balance was a mixture of new and old topsoil, containing numerous artifacts.

7C — An irregular intrusion of dark brown sandy loam with brick fragments and crumbs was removed. It contained bone, nails, ceramics, a pipe stem and glass and is associated with the posthole and post mold (7D and 7E) excavated in this unit.

NOTE: * designates photograph; + profile drawing; and # plan view.

126

PROVENIENCE NUMBER AND LOCATION	UNIT SIZE	DESCRIPTION AND WORK DONE
+7D		Removed a circular intrusion of dark brown sandy loam mixed with brick fragments. No artifacts except the brick fragments were found in this post mold. This mold and hole apparently are not associated with those found in Unit 6, as the difference in shape of the post indicates; 0.07 cubic foot of brick fragments were removed.
+7E		A circular intrusion of dark brown sandy loam mixed with brick crumbs and flecks and a heavy concentration of mortar was removed. This posthole measured 1.1' in diameter and was 1.4' deep. It contained a piece of dark green bottle glass and some bone, but it was not possible to establish a date for this feature.
*+#9B Mound		Below the sod and topsoil a level of dark brown sandy loam mottled with 50% marl crumbs and some brick flecks was removed. This was a thick, very hard-packed level of mound fill.
*+9C		Along the eastern edge of this unit a level of very dark gray brown clayey loam mottled with 10% light gray clay was removed. This is the same level of mound fill as that found in 5B.
*+#9D		Removed a layer of very dark brown clayey loam mottled with brick flecks and mortar and 50% light gray clay. This was an irregular series of lenticular fills forming part of the mound fill.
*+9E		Below the lenticular fill a level of dark brown sandy loam mottled with 5% brick flecks and 5% marl crumbs was removed over the northern half of the unit down to subsoil. This was the old topsoil and contained a large number of artifacts including ceramics, glass, nails, an iron key, slate and bone.

PROVENIENCE NUMBER AND LOCATION	UNIT SIZE	DECRIPTION AND WORK DONE

*+9F — Below the mound fill a level of very dark gray brown sandy loam mottled with 10% tan gray clayey loam was removed down to subsoil. This was a ditch that cut across the eastern end of the unit at an angle, being 1.7' wide on the north end and 2.6' wide at the south end. It contained some ceramics, glass and bone and is possibly a planting area connected with the rose garden, which was in this area before the mound.

*9G — Intruding through the old topsoil was a square post mold of very dark brown sandy loam mottled with 2% white sand. This is also most likely associated with the rose garden and stands only .5' from the ditch (9F).

+10A Trash Deposit 9' x 10' / +11A 9' x 10' — Removed a level of topsoil consisting of very dark gray brown sandy loam containing occasional brick, slate and roofing tile fragments.

+#10B / +#11B — Below the topsoil and distinguished from the 10A and 11A levels by the large quantities of rubble, a level of very dark gray brown sand loam was removed. This rubble level represented the destruction debris from a building and contained 7.2 cubic feet (218 quarts) of brick, 0.43 cubic feet (13 quarts) of slate, large quantities of roofing tile, plaster and mortar fragments. Also, many household artifacts were recovered, including more than 1,400 ceramic sherds, a brass pistol butt plate and many fragments of dark green bottle glass.

+10C / +11C — Below 10B and 11B removed a level of dark brown sandy loam mottled with oyster shell and marl crumbs. These areas also contained large quantities of household debris; the first of 3 George II young-head Irish halfpennies to be found in these excavations was discovered in 11C. The trash from this area dates from the last quarter of the 18th century.

NOTE: * designates photograph; + profile drawing; and # plan view.

128

PROVENIENCE NUMBER AND LOCATION	UNIT SIZE	DESCRIPTION AND WORK DONE
10D		Below 10C removed a rectangular intrusion of light gray clayey loam mottled with 40% tan yellow sandy loam and many marl crumbs. This area proved to be just an outcropping of the subsoil and contained no artifacts.
10E		Below 10C an irregular intrusion of dark brown sandy loam was removed from the southwest corner of the unit. From the irregularity of the feature, it was determined to be a root mold.
12A Miscellaneous	7.5' x 7.5'	Removed a level of sod and brick rubble composed of large brickbats and crushed brick down to dark brown sandy loam. This unit was never completed but was opened in the area where it was hoped to find the structure that generated the debris found in Units 10 and 11.
13 (not excavated) 14 " " 15 " "		
16A South Flanker	5' x 10'	Removed a level of sod and topsoil consisting of dark brown sandy loam that generally contained very few artifacts.
*+17A	7.5' x 7.5'	Removed a level of sod and topsoil consisting of dark brown sandy loam.
18A	7.5' x 8.75'	
+19A	7.5' x 7.5'	
20A	8.75' x 10'	
21A	1.25' x 7.5'	
22A	10' x 10'	
23A-26A	5' x 10'(each)	
27A	4' x 10'	
28A	10' x 10'	
16B		Removed a level of very dark brown sandy loam containing a small concentration of brick rubble in the northern portion of the unit. This area, full of household debris, represents the exterior destruction level of the south flanker.
*+17B		Below sod and topsoil removed a level of very dark gray brown sandy loam with occasional brick, plaster and mortar flecks. This was the level of destruction debris on the exterior of the flanker and contained large quantities of household debris including ceramics, glass, buttons, beads, bone and nails.

PROVENIENCE NUMBER AND LOCATION	UNIT SIZE	DESCRIPTION AND WORK DONE

#*+17C — Below sod and topsoil removed a level of dark brown sandy loam with occasional brickbats. This was the interior destruction level and in all cases was readily distinguishable from the exterior. It contained far more brick (3.4 cubic feet [103 quarts] interior vs. 0.3 cubic foot [10 quarts] exterior) and far fewer household goods.

+*17D — Below the level of interior rubble (17C), a level of dark brown sandy loam with 40% brickbats and brick crumbs and 30% mortar crumbs was removed. Only one straight pin and a prehistoric Indian pottery sherd were located in this level, which appeared to be an occupation level.

#*+17E — Below 17D removed a level of very dark brown sandy loam mixed with brickbats and brick crumbs and mortar fragments. This was the interior builder's trench and contained brick, a nail, charcoal, prehistoric ceramics and one piece of underglaze blue Chinese porcelain.

+17F — Below 17D removed a level of brown sandy loam mottled with 40% yellow brown clayey loam and 40% tan brown clayey loam with occasional brick and mortar crumbs.

*+17G — Below the exterior destruction debris (17B) removed a level of very dark gray sandy loam with 7% mortar crumbs and 80% oyster shell in the northeastern two-thirds. This was evidently an occupation level and contained numerous household goods.

*+#17H — A level of dark brown sandy loam with brick crumbs and mortar specks was removed. This was the exterior builder's trench and contained several sherds of prehistoric Indian pottery as well as some porcelain and a sherd of creamware.

NOTE: * designates photograph; + profile drawing; and # plan view.

130

PROVENIENCE NUMBER AND LOCATION	UNIT SIZE	DESCRIPTION AND WORK DONE

*+#17J

Below 17G a level of tan brown clay mottled with 10% dark gray brown sandy loam and occasional charcoal and brick flecks was removed. This clay was thought to have served to level this area in front of the flanker since the ground does slope noticeably from east to west. It contained household debris, including a diamond cut rhinestone.

*+#17K

A level of very dark brown sandy loam was removed from the flanker interior. This was the old topsoil level and contained only a few artifacts.

+17L

The exterior old topsoil level consisted of dark brown sandy loam mottled with 30% yellow clayey loam and a few oyster shells. Both the old topsoil levels were removed down to subsoil.

+17M

A circular intrusion of dark brown sandy loam mottled with 50% plaster and brick crumbs, intrusive through the old topsoil, was removed from the interior of the flanker. It contained no artifacts and was perhaps a floor support or scaffolding posthole.

*18B

Below the sod and topsoil a level of very dark gray brown sandy loam mixed with numerous brickbats and mortar fragments was removed. This level of destruction rubble contained more than 3.9 cubic feet (117 quarts) of brick and some ceramics, glass, bone, nails, a brass button and a thimble.

*#18C

This level of destruction debris was distinguished from level 18B by a difference in composition and compactness, this one being much more firmly compacted. It was a level of dark brown sandy loam mottled with 10% tan brown clayey loam mixed with numerous brickbats, brick crumbs, large mortar fragments and mortar crumbs. This level also contained household debris such as ceramics and glass. The 2nd Artillery button was recovered from this area. The brick made up the largest portion of this level, which averaged .6' in depth; 6.3 cubic feet (190 quarts) of brick were removed.

PROVENIENCE NUMBER AND LOCATION	UNIT SIZE	DESCRIPTION AND WORK DONE

*#18D

Along the eastern edge of this unit a shelf of mortar, consisting of loosely compacted mortar mixed with occasional brickbats, was removed. This contained only one sherd of creamware and one of clear bottle glass. This is the area that would have been within the chimney opening and may be associated with the chimney construction.

#18E

On the western edge of this unit a level of very dark brown sandy loam mixed with occasional brickbats and mortar flecks and two large patches of mortar was removed. The mortar and brick were associated with the destruction debris and the soil beneath, which contained a few ceramics, some glass, nails and bone and was the old topsoil level.

#18F

Below 18C removed a fill of bright red brown clayey sandy loam mixed with occasional brickbats. This was a very thin layer (about .2') and contained only a few artifacts. It is thought this level also was associated with the destruction of the chimney.

+#19B

Below the sod and topsoil a level of very dark gray brown sandy loam mixed with a heavy concentration of brickbats was removed. This area, on the exterior of the flanker, was destruction debris and contained a small quantity of household debris. 3.5 cubic feet (105 quarts) of brick were removed from this area. The western leg of the exterior entry stairway foundation was located in this level and hence the area of 19B would have been beneath the stairway.

+19C

A level of dark brown sandy loam with a heavy concentration of brickbats in the western one-third, occasional brickbats over the other two-thirds and 30% mortar specks overall was removed beneath the sod and topsoil. This was the interior destruction level and contained only 1.2 cubic feet (36 quarts) of brick. The north leg and northwest corner of the chimney foundation were uncovered in this area.

NOTE: * designates photograph; + profile drawing; and # plan view.

PROVENIENCE NUMBER AND LOCATION	UNIT SIZE	DESCRIPTION AND WORK DONE

#19D — Below the destruction debris on the interior of the flanker, a level of dark brown sandy loam mottled with 10% tan brown clayey loam and mixed with occasional brick flecks was removed. This was an extremely thin level, containing only bone, prehistoric Indian pottery, two pipe stems and some bone. It is thought that this may represent a very thin level of occupational debris.

+19E — Below the occupational fill (19D) a level of dark brown sandy loam mottled with 30% tan brown clayey loam mixed with occasional brick and mortar crumbs was removed. Only six artifacts were recovered and it is possible that this level represents construction debris.

*+#19F — The interior builder's trench, consisting of very dark brown sandy loam mottled with 30% yellow brown sandy loam and occasional brick and mortar flecks, was excavated. Five prehistoric Indian sherds and some bone were the only artifacts recovered.

*+#19G — A level of very dark brown sandy loam mottled with 20% mortar flecks and occasional brickbats was removed. This was the exterior builder's trench and, like the interior one, contained only a few artifacts.

*19H — A posthole, intrusive through the construction ditch, was excavated on the exterior of the flanker. It consisted of very dark brown sandy loam mixed with occasional brick and mortar flecks. It was .63' deep and contained ceramics, including a piece of whiteware, glass and bone.

*#19J — Below the construction debris (19E), removed a level of dark brown sandy loam mottled with 40% tan brown clayey loam and 20% tan yellow clayey sand. Only one piece of mortar was recovered in this area and it is possible that this feature is associated with the chimney or foundation construction as it lies between the two.

PROVENIENCE NUMBER AND LOCATION	UNIT SIZE	DESCRIPTION AND WORK DONE
*+19K		Below 19E removed a level of dark brown sandy loam mottled with 30% dark gray brown sandy loam, 10% tan brown clayey loam, 10% tan yellow clayey loam and occasional brick and mortar flecks which contained a few artifacts and seemed to represent a cap of fill over the area.
*+19L		A level of dark brown sandy loam was removed to a depth of more than 2' before reaching subsoil. It contained only ceramics, mainly prehistoric ones, and was on the interior of the flanker.
*19M		A level of very dark brown sandy loam was removed down to subsoil, which, as in 19L, was more than 2' down. These two features were separated by the flanker foundation wall, which had no break in it at that point. This was also the area that would have been under the exterior stairway. From the depth and irregularity of the feature, it is thought that this and 19L represent a large tree-root mold, the tree and stump having been removed and the hole filled prior to construction.
20B 20B, extended		Below sod and topsoil a level of very dark gray brown sandy loam mixed with mortar flecks was removed. This area, which was outside the entry stairway on the exterior of the south flanker, contained large quantities of household debris and nails but only .5 cubic foot (16 quarts) of brick. This unit, originally 7.5' x 10', was extended an additional 1.25' to the north because the angle of the flanker foundation through the unit was such that there was insufficient working space.
20C 20C, extended		This area, inside the stairway foundation, consisted of dark gray brown sandy loam mixed with mortar flecks and a heavy concentration of brickbats. Like 19B, it contained more brick than household debris and would have been beneath the stairway foundation. 1.6 cubic feet (48 quarts) were removed.

NOTE: * designates photograph; + profile drawing; and # plan view.

PROVENIENCE NUMBER AND LOCATION	UNIT SIZE	DESCRIPTION AND WORK DONE

20D

The interior rubble fill, consisting of dark brown sandy loam mixed with a moderate concentration of brickbats and 20% mortar flecks, was removed. Ceramics, glass and bone, along with 2. cubic feet (61 quarts) were taken from this level of destruction debris.

*#20E

Below 20B a level of dark brown sandy loam mixed with occasional brick flecks was removed. This appeared to be an area of occupational debris and contained large quantities of household debris.

*#20F

The interior builder's trench was removed from this area. It consisted of a light gray brown sandy loam mottled with 5% tan brown clayey loam and occasional brick and mortar flecks. It contained one fragment of tin-glazed earthenware, a nail and some bone and reached the subsoil at a depth of more than 1'.

*#20G

Below the exterior destruction rubble (20C) removed a level of dark brown sandy loam mottled with 10% tan brown clayey loam and 10% yellow brown clayey loam with occasional brick and mortar flecks. Very few artifacts were recovered from this level, which may represent a construction area for the stairway.

#21B

Unit 21 was the 1.25' balk left between Units 20 and 19 when it was discovered that the end of the chimney foundation (north leg) underlay this area. Level 21B consisted of very dark gray brown sandy loam mixed with brickbats and crumbs and was more of the exterior destruction debris (see 17B, 20B, 22B).

21C

Below the sod and topsoil a level of very dark brown sandy loam mixed with numerous brickbats and brick crumbs was removed. This was the interior destruction debris similar to that found in 17C, 19C and 20D.

*#21D

The interior builder's trench, consisting of dark brown sandy loam with occasional brick crumbs and mortar flecks, was removed down to subsoil. It contained two pieces of prehistoric Indian pottery and one wrought nail.

PROVENIENCE NUMBER AND LOCATION	UNIT SIZE	DESCRIPTION AND WORK DONE

21E

Below the interior destruction debris a thin level of dark brown sandy loam mottled with 10% tan brown clayey loam was removed. No artifacts were found in this level, which was possibly deposited during the occupational period.

*#21F

This level of dark brown sandy loam mottled with 40% tan brown clayey loam and 20% tan yellow clayey sand is the same as 19J, and like that level, it contained no artifacts but is most likely associated with construction activity.

*#21G

This posthole, consisting of a square intrusion of dark brown sandy loam mottled with 10% tan brown sandy loam was removed down to subsoil. It contained a few pieces of glass, bone and ceramics. A circular depression at the bottom of the hole indicated the removal of a post, but no post mold was visible in the posthole. This posthole is placed between the builder's trench and the chimney foundation and is most likely the result of scaffolding erected for the construction of the building and/or the chimney.

22B

Below the sod and topsoil a level of very dark gray brown sandy loam was removed. This was the area of destruction debris outside the flanker foundation and contained very large amounts of household trash but very little brick.

22C

The interior destruction rubble, consisting of very dark brown sandy loam mottled with 30% tan brown clayey loam mixed with numerous brickbats and crumbs was removed. As in previous cases, the interior contained far fewer artifacts but large quantities of brick (85 quarts).

22D

Below 22C removed a level of dark brown sandy loam with numerous brickbats, mortar crumbs and occasional pockets of crushed brick and sand. This level, which contained three porcelain fragments and a flat piece of iron, is possibly associated with the occupation of the flanker.

NOTE: * designates photograph; + profile drawing; and # plan view.

136

PROVENIENCE NUMBER AND LOCATION	UNIT SIZE	DESCRIPTION AND WORK DONE

#22E

A level of very dark brown sandy loam mottled with 20% tan brown sandy loam and mixed with occasional brickbats and crumbs and mortar flecks was removed below 22D. Only three pottery fragments were recovered, including a sherd of North Devonshire gravel-tempered earthenware. This level is most likely associated with the flanker construction.

#22F

On the northeast interior corner of the flanker, a square intrusion of dark brown sandy loam mottled with 10% tan brown sandy loam was removed. This intrusion overlay the builder's trench and contained only one piece of dark green bottle glass. It was very shallow and is possibly related to the period of occupation or destruction.

*#22G

Removed a rectangular intrusion of very dark gray brown sandy loam mottled with 30% tan brown sandy loam mixed with brick fragments and mortar crumbs. The rectangular shape immediately changed and became very irregular; it is apparent that this is a root mold. No artifacts were found.

*#22H

The interior construction ditch in Unit 22 consisted of dark brown sandy loam mottled with 20% tan brown sandy loam with occasional brickbats and crumbs and mortar flecks with a heavy concentration of crushed brick and mortar. There were only a few artifacts recovered, including a piece of tin-glazed earthenware, but an unusual amount of brick and mortar--1 cubic foot (31 quarts) was removed.

*#22J

Removed a level of dark gray brown sandy loam down to subsoil. This was the old topsoil level and contained prehistoric Indian pottery, white clay pipe stem fragments and some bone.

#22K

Below the exterior destruction fill a level of very dark brown sandy loam mixed with brick fragments and occasional mortar flecks was removed. This was found along the north flanker foundation wall, bounded by the connector wall at the northeast corner. This was possibly an area of occupational debris.

| PROVENIENCE NUMBER AND LOCATION | UNIT SIZE | DESCRIPTION AND WORK DONE |

*22L (not excavated)

#22M — Removed a square intrusion of yellow brown clayey loam mottled with 20% dark brown clayey loam and mixed with brick and oyster shell dust. This was the post mold from a post placed in the flanker corner during occupation or destruction. Like the post-hole (22F), it was very shallow and overlay the construction ditch. Four fish bones, an egg shell fragment and a piece of iron scrap were the only artifacts recovered.

*#22N — Below the exterior destruction rubble a level of dark brown sandy loam mottled with 30% dark gray brown clayey loam, brickbats, brick and mortar flecks, oyster shell and charcoal fragments was removed. This was a trash disposal area concentrated along the eastern wall of the flanker and contained large amounts of household debris.

*23B — This was a level of exterior destruction debris along the west wall of the flanker and contained large quantities of ceramics, glass, nails and bone. The level was a very dark gray brown sandy loam.

24-28 (not opened beyond the "A" level)

29-31 (not opened)

Provenience	Location	Unit Size
32A	Test Trenches	2.5' x 12.85'
33A	between Flan-	2.5' x 14.14'
+34A	ker and House	2.5' x 14.14'
*+35A		2.5' x 4.6'
36A		2.5' x 14.14'
37A		2.5' x 14.14'

Removed a level of sod and topsoil consisting of very dark brown sandy loam. This level contained a variety of artifacts ranging from the older ceramic types to modern debris, including a sardine can lid. These areas represent a series of test trenches placed between the main house and the flanker in an effort to locate the connector.

32B, 33B, +34B, *+35B, 36B, 37B — Below the sod and topsoil removed a level of dark brown sandy loam mixed with a scattering of brick crumbs and mortar. These units all contained a large quantity of household debris, but the amount increased as the units moved toward the house. The connector wall was uncovered at the southeastern end of Unit 36.

NOTE: * designates photograph; + profile drawing; and # plan view.

PROVENIENCE NUMBER AND LOCATION	UNIT SIZE	DESCRIPTION AND WORK DONE
32C 33C +34C 35G		Below the level of occupational debris, a level of very dark brown sandy loam mottled with 15-25% yellow brown clayey loam. This was the old topsoil level, representing original grade, and contained smaller quantities of household debris.
32D +37D		Below the old topsoil removed a level composed of 50% very dark brown sandy loam and 50% yellow brown clayey loam. This was the subsoil level in this area, which was checked for the first half foot; it contained only one prehistoric Indian sherd.
34D		Removed an irregular intrusion of very dark reddish brown sandy loam. This feature contained several large pieces of a restorable feather-edge creamware platter, a flat lead scrap, glass fragments, charcoal, brick and mortar flecks. It was .6' deep and its function has not been identified.
*+35C #38C		Below the sod and topsoil removed a narrow layer of brown sandy loam mottled with 75% very light gray sand and red particles. This was the drip line from the roof of the house. The red matter in the soil was from the red paint on the roof. Found in this feature were large amounts of window glass along with ceramics and bottle glass.
*+35D #38D		Removed a level of very dark brown sandy loam that was extremely loosely compacted. This was a portion of the trenching done for termite control purposes and contained glass, ceramics, nails and a lead finial.
+35E		Below 35D removed a square intrusion of dark brown sandy loam mottled with 25% yellow brown clayey loam and 25% tan brown clayey loam down to a brick floor. This was apparently the hole into which the downspout was inserted, draining off onto the brick flooring beneath. It had been packed with all manner of artifacts, particularly dark green wine bottle glass.

PROVENIENCE NUMBER AND LOCATION	UNIT SIZE	DESCRIPTION AND WORK DONE

+#35F

Below 35D removed a level of dark brown sandy loam mottled with 15% brick crumbs and fleck down to the brick floor. This level contained ceramics, glass, nails, mortar and brick and appeared to be a fill or construction rubble over the brick floor.

36C
*+41D

Removed an irregular intrusion of very dark brown sandy loam mottled with 25% mortar and 25% brick fragments with a scattering of oyster shell. This area contained a restorable portion of a white salt-glazed stoneware teapot including the handle. At one point in the level, there was an almost solid layer of mortar.

36D

A level of very dark brown sandy loam mottled with 10% yellow brown clayey loam was removed down to the subsoil. This was the old topsoil level which contained some bone, nails and ceramics.

36E
*+41E

Below 36C and 41D removed a level of dark yellow brown clayey loam mottled with 15% very dark brown sandy loam, 10% light gray clay and 10% yellow brown clay with a heavy concentration of oyster shell and numerous brickbats. White salt-glazed stoneware, dark green bottle glass and a large poorly preserved fragment of tin-glazed earthenware were found in this semicircular intrusion. This, together with the level immediately above, seems to compose a materials staging area for the construction of the connector and/or the house and flanker.

36F

Below the old topsoil level (36D) a semicircular intrusion of very dark brown sandy loam with 10% brick fragments and a high concentration of clay. No artifacts were recovered. This area appears to be associated with the 36C, 41D, 36E and 41E areas. The clay in this pit resembles raw brick clay and chinking of the same material has been found in the attic of the main house.

NOTE: * designates photograph; + profile drawing; and # plan view.

140

PROVENIENCE NUMBER AND LOCATION	UNIT SIZE	DESCRIPTION AND WORK DONE
37C		Removed a level of very dark brown sandy loam mottled with 10% yellow brown clayey loam down to subsoil. This was the old topsoil level and contained only a few artifacts.
38A Triangle +41A Connector 42A	30.1'x 21.775' x 18.125' 55 square feet 25 square feet	Removed a level of sod and topsoil consisting of dark brown sandy loam from these areas. Units 41 and 42 were quite irregular in shape and square footage was determined rather than perimeter dimension. These sod and topsoil levels contained a mixture of debris that included modern soda bottle glass and early ceramic types.
#38B		Below the sod and topsoil removed a level of dark brown sandy loam with extremely heavy concentrations of household debris including ceramics, glass, buttons, nails, pins, pipe stems and bowls and furniture. The George III Irish halfpenny was recovered from this area. The occupational debris represented by this level had an average thickness of .56'.
#38E #38F		Removed two square intrusions of yellow brown clayey loam. Both were extremely shallow and contained no artifacts (35E was .02' and 35F was .05'). It was thought at first that these were postholes, but on excavation they appeared to have been just small depressions in the old topsoil level.
38G		Below 38B removed a circular intrusion of very dark brown sandy loam mottled with 50% mortar and plaster. This area contained nails, window glass and one bead and appeared to be a splash of mortar overlying feature 38J.
*38H		Below 38B removed a rectangular intrusion of dark yellow brown clayey loam mixed with brick and mortar crumbs. Artifacts included numerous fragments of a white salt-glazed stoneware chamber pot, one sherd of pearlware, window and bottle glass, nails and bone.

PROVENIENCE NUMBER
AND LOCATION   UNIT SIZE   DESCRIPTION AND WORK DONE

*38J

Below 38H removed a level of very dark brown sandy loam mottled with 20% dark yellow brown clayey loam and 20% tan brown clayey loam. This rectangular feature was evidently filled in two stages, 38H representing the upper fill level. The artifacts were similar. At the bottom of this feature the crow's foot lightning rod ground was located.

*38K

A circular intrusion of very dark brown sandy loam mottled with 20% tan brown clayey loam and occasional brick flecks was removed. This feature was intrusive into feature 38J and is a posthole that contained glass, brick flecks and nails.

38L

Below 38D removed a level of very dark brown sandy loam (normal compaction) that contained ceramics, glass, nails, beads, a pewter spoon handle, goblet fragments and lead shot. This was part of the occupational debris underlying the area disturbed by the termite control trench.

38M

An irregular intrusion of very dark brown sandy loam with two large iron fragments protruding from it was removed. This feature was just north of feature 38J and was part of it, the two iron pieces eventually connecting to the perpendicular of the lightning rod ground.

38N

Below 38L removed a level of very dark brown sandy loam, the old topsoil level, which was very thin at this point and overlay the exterior builder's trench for the main house.

38P

Below 38L removed a circular intrusion of very dark brown sandy loam that was very loosely compacted. This circular hole angled to the south and joined feature 38J, being a part of the lightning rod ground.

38Q

Below the north end of feature 38J removed a circular intrusion of very dark gray brown clayey loam, down to subsoil. This feature contained creamware, white salt-glazed stoneware, glass, nails and pipe stem and was also associated with the lightning rod complex.

NOTE: * designates photograph; + profile drawing; and # plan view.

PROVENIENCE NUMBER AND LOCATION	UNIT SIZE	DESCRIPTION AND WORK DONE
39A Ground Floor Central Room	.55' x 2.35'	Below the stone floor of the central ground-level room removed a mixture of crushed oyster shell and dark yellow brown clayey loam. The oyster shell apparently had been used to level the floor before the laying of the paving stones.
*40A	10.86 sq.ft.	Removed a level of paving stones in front of the doorway into the southwest room on the ground floor of the main house.
*40B		Below the paving stones removed a level of mortar mottled with 50% brick dust and traces of very dark brown sandy loam and disturbance by rodent burrowing. This level consisted of mortar placed under the cracked paving stones to effect repairs and level the cracked stones.
*40C		Below the paving stones and mortar layer a level of light tan brown sand mottled with 5% brick flecks was removed. This was apparently a leveling fill deposited before the laying of the paving stones.
*40D		Below 40C removed several intrusions of very dark brown sandy loam mottled with 10% brick and 10% mortar fragments and 50% light tan brown sand. These areas were rodent burrows and contained oyster shell, glass, nails, ceramics and bones.
*40E		This was a circular intrusion that appeared to be a posthole initially but on excavation proved to be part of the rodent burrow complex.
*40F		Removed a level of medium brown sandy loam mottled with 25% tan brown sand, 20% brick dust and crumbs and 15% mortar crumbs down to the builder's trench along the wall and old topsoil in front of the doorway. This appears to be occupational debris that was deposited before the floor was paved with stone.

PROVENIENCE NUMBER AND LOCATION	UNIT SIZE	DESCRIPTION AND WORK DONE
*#41B Connector *#42B		Beneath the sod and topsoil removed a level of very dark gray brown sandy loam. Removal of this level exposed the remains of the connecting wall, running from the northeast corner of the south flanker to the southwest corner of the main house. It was two courses wide and in many places had been destroyed by tree-root action. The artifacts included glass and ceramics, along with some nails.
*+41C		Below the sod and topsoil removed a level of very dark gray brown sandy loam. This thin occupational level contained ceramics, nails, glass, a brass button, a spoon handle and pipe bowl fragments.
*+41F		Below 41E removed a level of orange brown clayey sand mottled with 10% tan brown clayey sand and 40% brown clay down to the level of subsoil. This fill underlay the materials staging area (41D and 41E) and was similar to the fill found in feature 36F. No artifacts were found.
43A Lawn Test Area 44A	5' x 8.6' 5' x 6.75'	Removed a level of sod and topsoil consisting of dark brown sandy loam. Modern trash along with wire nails and ceramics were found in this area.
43B		Below the sod and topsoil removed a level of dark brown sandy loam mottled with 10% charcoal flecks. Whiteware and pearlware, along with nails and glass, were recovered from this area.
43C		Removed an irregular intrusion of dark brown sandy loam mixed with 50% charcoal crumbs. From the bricks exposed at the top of this feature, it was thought it might be a chimney foundation; however, it was a circular area of brick, evidently used for burning 20th century trash. This was evidenced by the appearance of several pieces of burned asphalt shingle and pieces of tin roofing.

NOTE: * designates photograph; + profile drawing; and # plan view.

144

PROVENIENCE NUMBER AND LOCATION	UNIT SIZE	DESCRIPTION AND WORK DONE
+45A	2' x 19.2'	Removed a level of sod and topsoil consisting of dark brown sandy loam. No artifacts were found. The entire 19.2-foot-long trench was cut across the serpentine area as a test to determine if this was the ha-ha referred to in Charles Drayton's diary. It consisted of a series of lenticular fills in such a manner that it appeared to be a flower bed and not the ornamental ditch.

APPENDIX D: MEAN CERAMIC DATE COMPUTATIONS

The Mean Ceramic Dating formula used is that one presented by South (1972) as
modified and used in Palmetto Parapets (South 1974). To use the South formula,
a median date is first derived from the beginning and terminal dates of
manufacture for particular ceramic types. The dates are based on Noel Hume's
discussion of ceramics in A Guide to Artifacts of Colonial America (1970), as
later modified and presented by South (1972:85). The number of sherds (sherd
count) of each ceramic type is multiplied by the median date, creating a
product. The total of all the sherds is then divided into the total of all
the products, thus providing a raw mean ceramic date for that particular
group of ceramics. This date is further modified by using the formula

$$Z = 235.5 + .87Y$$

where Y (the mean ceramic date) is derived using the formula

$$Y = \frac{\sum_{i=1}^{n} \cdot X_i \cdot f_i}{\sum_{i=1}^{n} f_i}$$

X_i = median date for the manufacture
of each ceramic type

f_i = the frequency of each ceramic
type

n = the number of ceramic types
in the sample

thus providing a median occupation date. It should be borne in mind that this
date is only a measure of central tendency for any given site or area of a
site and is not an absolute date. It must be used in conjunction with other
information about a deposit to provide an accurate picture of the occupation
period reflected by the ceramics and other materials present in it.

146

TABLE 1
Units 10 and 11 - Trash Deposit (10B, C, D, E; 11B, 11C)

Ceramic Type	Type Median	Sherd Count	Product
Overglaze enameled China trade porcelain	1808	33	59,664
English porcelain	1770	1	1,770
Brown stoneware bottles for ink, beer, etc.	1860	2	3,720
Nottingham stoneware	1755	1	1,755
British brown stoneware	1733	11	19,063
Westerwald, stamped blue floral devices, geometric designs	1738	19	33,022
Moulded white salt-glazed stoneware	1753	2	3,506
White salt-glazed stoneware	1763	13	22,919
White salt-glazed stoneware plates	1758	4	7,032
Slip-dipped white salt-glazed stoneware	1745	1	1,745
"Black basaltes" stoneware	1785	6	10,710
Lead-glazed slipware (combed yellow)	1733	136	235,688
Whiteware	1860	6	11,160
Mocha	1843	1	1,843
"Jackfield" ware	1760	1	1,760
Everted rim, undecorated tin-enameled ware ointment pot (delft)	1750	3	5,250
18th-century decorated tin-enameled ware (delft)	1750	2	3,500
Undecorated tin-enameled ware wash basins (delft)	1775	7	12,425
Undecorated white tin-enameled ware (delft)	1720	15	25,800
"Finger-painted" wares (polychrome slip on creamware or pearlware)	1805	5	9,025

TABLE 1, continued

Ceramic Type	Type Median	Sherd Count	Product
"Annular wares" creamware	1798	5	8,990
Creamware	1791	598	1,071,018
Transfer-printed pearlware	1818	83	150,894
Underglaze polychrome pearlware, directly stenciled	1830	38	69,540
"Annular wares" pearlware	1805	36	64,980
Underglaze blue hand-painted pearlware	1800	27	48,600
Blue and green-edged pearlware	1805	32	57,760
Undecorated pearlware	1805	73	131,765
Total		1,161	2,074,904

Ceramic Formula Computation

2074904 ÷ 1161 = 1787.2 x .87 = 1554.8 + 235.5 = 1790.3

TABLE 2
Units 17, 19, 20, 21, 22 - South Flanker Exterior Destruction Debris
(17B, 19B, 20B, 20C, 21B, 22B)

Ceramic Type	Type Median	Sherd Count	Product
Overglaze enameled China trade porcelain	1808	30	54,240
English porcelain	1770	2	3,540
Brown stoneware bottles for ink, beer, etc.	1860	7	13,020
Nottingham stoneware	1755	1	1,755
British brown stoneware	1733	8	13,864

148

TABLE 2, continued

Ceramic Type	Type Median	Sherd Count	Product
Westerwald, stamped blue floral devices, geometric designs	1738	3	5,214
Moulded white salt-glazed stoneware	1753	2	3,506
White salt-glazed stoneware	1763	7	12,341
White salt-glazed stoneware plates	1758	5	8,790
"Black basaltes" stoneware	1785	1	1,785
Engine-turned unglazed red stoneware	1769	1	1,769
Lead-glazed slipware (combed yellow)	1733	70	121,310
Whiteware	1860	30	55,800
Mocha	1843	3	5,529
"Jackfield" ware	1760	5	8,800
Buckley ware	1748	5	8,740
18th-century decorated tin-enameled ware (delft)	1750	18	31,500
Undecorated tin-enameled wash basins (delft)	1775	1	1,775
Undecorated white tin-enameled ware (delft)	1720	18	30,960
"Finger-painted" wares (polychrome slip on creamware or pearlware)	1805	1	1,805
"Annular wares" creamware	1798	17	30,566
Enameled hand-painted creamware	1788	2	3,576
Creamware	1791	251	449,541
Underglaze polychrome pearlware, directly stenciled	1830	7	12,810
Transfer-printed pearlware	1818	21	38,178
"Annular wares" pearlware	1805	38	68,590

TABLE 2, continued

Ceramic Type	Type Median	Sherd Count	Product
Underglaze blue hand-painted pearlware	1800	6	10,800
Blue and green-edged pearlware	1805	4	7,220
Undecorated pearlware	1805	38	68,590
Total		602	1,075,914

Ceramic Formula Computation

1, 075, 914 ÷ 602 = 1787.2 x .87 = 1554.9 +235.5 = 1790.4

TABLE 3
Units 17, 18, 19, 20, 21, 22 - South Flanker Interior Destruction Debris
(17C, 18B, 18C, 19C, 20D, 21C, 22C)

Ceramic Type	Type Median	Sherd Count	Product
Overglaze enameled China trade porcelain	1808	3	5,424
English porcelain	1770	2	3,540
Nottingham stoneware	1755	2	3,510
British brown stoneware	1733	1	1,733
Westerwald, stamped blue floral devices, geometric designs	1738	7	12,166
Moulded white salt-glazed stoneware	1753	4	7,012
White salt-glazed stoneware	1763	1	1,763
White salt-glazed stoneware plates	1758	1	1,758
Lead-glazed slipware (combed yellow)	1733	10	17,330
Whiteware	1860	5	9,300

150

TABLE 3, continued

Ceramic Type	Type Median	Sherd Count	Product
"Clouded" wares, tortoiseshell, mottled glazed cream-colored ware	1755	2	3,510
Buckley ware	1748	1	1,748
Everted rim, undecorated tin-enameled ointment pot (delft)	1750	3	5,250
18th-century decorated tin-enameled ware (delft)	1750	6	10,500
Undecorated white tin-enameled ware (delft)	1720	4	6,880
"Finger-painted" wares (polychrome slip on creamware or pearlware)	1805	3	5,415
Enameled hand-painted creamware	1788	1	1,788
Creamware	1791	12	21,492
Transfer-printed pearlware	1818	5	9,090
"Annular wares" pearlware	1805	11	19,855
Blue and green-edged pearlware	1805	3	5,415
Undecorated pearlware	1805	29	52,345
Total		116	206,824

Ceramic Formula Computation

206,824 ÷ 116 = 1783 x .87 = 1551.2 + 235.5 = 1786.7

TABLE 4
Units 17G, 20E, 22K, 22N - Exterior Occupation Levels

Ceramic Type	Type Median	Sherd Count	Product
Overglaze enameled China trade porcelain	1808	14	25,312

TABLE 4, continued

Ceramic Type	Type Median	Sherd Count	Product
English porcelain	1770	3	5,310
British brown stoneware	1733	2	3,466
Westerwald chamber pots	1738	1	1,738
Westerwald, stamped blue floral devices, geometric designs	1738	4	6,952
Moulded white salt-glazed stoneware	1753	1	1,753
White salt-glazed stoneware	1763	5	8,815
"Black basaltes" stoneware	1785	3	5,355
Lead-glazed slipware (combed yellow)	1733	22	38,126
Whiteware	1860	1	1,860
Mocha	1843	1	1,843
"Jackfield" ware	1760	2	3,520
"Clouded" wares, tortoiseshell, mottled glazed cream-colored ware	1755	1	1,755
Refined agateware	1758	1	1,758
Everted rim, undecorated tin-enameled ointment pot (delft)	1750	1	1,750
18th-century decorated tin-enameled ware (delft)	1750	13	22,750
Undecorated white tin-enameled ware (delft)	1720	4	6,880
"Finger-painted" wares (polychrome slip on creamware or pearlware)	1805	3	5,415
"Annular wares" creamware	1798	2	3,596
Creamware	1791	101	180,891
Underglaze polychrome pearlware directly stenciled	1830	2	3,660
Transfer-printed pearlware	1818	8	14,544

152

TABLE 4, continued

Ceramic Type	Type Median	Sherd Count	Product
"Annular wares" pearlware	1805	11	19,855
Underglaze blue hand-painted pearlware	1800	13	23,400
Blue and green-edged pearlware	1805	3	5,415
Undecorated pearlware	1805	28	50,540
Total		250	446,259

Ceramic Formula Computation

446,259 ÷ 250 = 1785   x .87 = 1553 + 235.5 = 1788.5

TABLE 5
Units 41B and 42B - Connector

Ceramic Type	Type Median	Sherd Count	Product
Overglaze enameled China trade porcelain	1808	4	7,232
English porcelain	1770	1	1,770
White salt-glazed stoneware	1763	40	70,520
White salt-glazed stoneware plates	1758	5	8,790
Engine-turned unglazed red stoneware	1769	2	3,538
Lead-glazed slipware (combed yellow)	1733	8	13,864
Whiteware	1860	1	1,860
18th-century decorated tin-enameled ware	1750	1	1,750
"Finger-painted" wares (polychrome slip on creamware or pearlware)	1805	3	5,415
Creamware	1791	26	46,566

153

TABLE 5, continued

Ceramic Type	Type Median	Sherd Count	Product
Transfer-printed pearlware	1818	16	29,088
"Annular wares" pearlware	1805	1	1,805
Underglaze blue hand-painted pearlware	1800	1	1,800
Blue and green-edged pearlware	1805	1	1,805
Undecorated pearlware	1805	5	9,025
Total		115	204,833

Ceramic Formula Computation

204,833 ÷ 115 = 1781.2 x .87 = 1549.6 + 235.5 = 1785.1

TABLE 6
Main House (38J)

Ceramic Type	Type Median	Sherd Count	Product
Overglaze enameled China trade porcelain	1808	7	12,656
British brown stoneware	1733	2	3,466
Westerwald, stamped blue floral devices, geometric designs	1738	2	3,476
Moulded white salt-glazed stoneware	1753	1	1,753
White salt-glazed stoneware	1763	72	126,936
"Black basaltes" stoneware	1785	1	1,785
Lead-glazed slipware (combed yellow)	1733	2	3,466
"Finger-painted" wares (polychrome slip on creamware or pearlware)	1805	2	3,610
Creamware	1791	16	28,656

154

TABLE 6, continued

Ceramic Type	Type Median	Sherd Count	Product
Transfer-printed pearlware	1818	2	3,636
Undecorated pearlware	1805	5	9,025
Total		112	198,465

Ceramic Formula Computation

198,465 ÷ 112 = 1772 x .87 = 1541.6 + 235.5 = 1777.1

TABLE 7
Unit 38, House Occupation (38B, C, D, H, L and N)
Summary of Mean Ceramic Dates

Unit	Mean Ceramic Date
38B	1799.7
38C	1790.5
38D	1795.3
38H	1796.6
38L	1796.1
38N	1785.3

Average Mean Ceramic Date: 1793.9

TABLE 8
38B - Summary

Unit	Mean Ceramic Date
38B Ia	1787.4

TABLE 8, continued

Unit	Mean Ceramic Date
38B II	1799.4
38B IIa	1801.4
38B III	1808.0
38B IIIa	1797.5
38B IV	1802.5
38B IVa	1797.8
38B V	1802.7
38B Va	1805.9
38B VI	1794.3

Average Mean Ceramic Date: 1799.7

TABLE 9
38B Ia

Ceramic Type	Type Median	Sherd Count	Product
British brown stoneware	1733	1	1,733
White salt-glazed stoneware	1763	5	8,815
Lead-glazed slipware (combed yellow)	1733	15	25,995
"Clouded" wares, tortoiseshell, mottled glazed cream-colored ware	1755	4	7,020
North Devon gravel-tempered ware	1713	4	6,852
Everted rim, undecorated tin-enameled ointment pot (delft)	1750	1	1,750
Creamware	1791	56	100,296

156

TABLE 9, continued

Ceramic Type	Type Median	Sherd Count	Product
Underglazed polychrome pearlware directly stenciled	1830	5	9,150
Transfer-printed pearlware	1818	11	19,998
"Annular wares" pearlware	1805	2	3,610
Underglaze blue hand-painted pearlware	1800	1	1,800
Blue and green-edged pearlware	1805	1	1,805
Undecorated pearlware	1805	12	21,660
Total		118	210,484

Ceramic Formula Computation

210,484 ÷ 118 = 1783.8 x .87 = 1551.9 + 235.5 = 1787.3

TABLE 10
38B II

Ceramic Type	Type Median	Sherd Count	Product
Overglaze enameled China trade porcelain	1808	1	1,808
Engine-turned unglazed red stoneware	1769	6	10,614
Lead-glazed slipware (combed yellow)	1733	1	1,733
Whiteware	1860	3	5,580
Creamware	1791	2	3,582
Transfer-printed pearlware	1818	1	1,818

TABLE 10, continued

Ceramic Type	Type Median	Sherd Count	Product
"Annular wares" pearlware	1805	1	1,805
Underglaze blue hand-painted pearlware	1800	1	1,800
Undecorated pearlware	1805	3	5,415
Total		19	34,155

Ceramic Formula Computation

$34,155 \div 19 = 1797.6 \times .87 = 1563.9 + 235.5 = 1799.4$

TABLE 11
38B IIa

Ceramic Type	Type Median	Sherd Count	Product
Overglaze enameled China trade porcelain	1808	1	1,808
English porcelain	1770	3	5,310
White salt-glazed stoneware	1763	4	7,052
Engine-turned unglazed red stoneware	1769	3	5,307
Lead-glazed slipware (combed yellow)	1733	3	5,199
Whiteware	1860	4	7,440
Mocha	1843	2	3,686
"Clouded" Wares, tortoiseshell, mottled glazed cream-colored ware	1755	1	1,755
North Devon gravel-tempered ware	1713	2	3,426
Undecorated white tin-enameled ware (delft)	1720	1	1,720

TABLE 11, continued

Ceramic Type	Type Median	Sherd Count	Product
"Finger-painted" wares (polychrome slip on creamware or pearlware)	1805	10	18,050
"Annular wares" creamware	1798	1	1,798
Enameled hand-painted creamware	1788	4	7,152
Creamware	1791	76	136,116
Underglazed polychrome pearlware, directly stenciled	1830	2	3,660
Embossed pearlware	1810	2	3,620
Transfer-printed pearlware	1818	45	81,810
Underglaze polychrome pearlware	1805	8	14,440
"Annular wares" pearlware	1805	2	3,610
Blue and green-edged pearlware	1805	11	19,855
Undecorated pearlware	1805	32	57,760
Total		217	390,574

Ceramic Formula Computation

$394,094 \div 219 = 1799.5 \times .87 = 1565.6 + 235.5 = 1801.1$

TABLE 12
38B III

Ceramic Type	Type Median	Sherd Count	Product
Littler's blue	1758	2	3,516
Engine-turned unglazed red stoneware	1769	4	7,076

TABLE 12, continued

Ceramic Type	Type Median	Sherd Count	Product
Whiteware	1860	6	11,160
Mocha	1843	1	1,843
"Clouded" wares, tortoiseshell, mottled glazed cream-colored ware	1755	2	3,510
Creamware	1791	6	10,746
Transfer-printed pearlware	1818	12	21,816
"Annular wares" pearlware	1805	3	5,415
Undecorated pearlware	1805	5	9,025
Total		41	74,107

Ceramic Formula Computation

74,024 ÷ 41 = 1805.5 x .87 = 1570.7 + 235.5 = 1806.2

TABLE 13
38B IIIa

Ceramic Type	Type Median	Sherd Count	Product
Overglaze enameled China trade porcelain	1808	27	48,816
English porcelain	1770	7	12,390
Littler's blue	1758	2	3,516
Nottingham stoneware	1755	3	5,265
British brown stoneware	1733	2	3,466
White salt-glazed stoneware	1763	42	74,046
Engine-turned unglazed red stoneware	1769	10	17,690

160

TABLE 13, continued

Ceramic Type	Type Median	Sherd Count	Product
Lead-glazed slipware (combed yellow)	1733	3	5,199
Whiteware	1860	8	14,880
Mocha	1843	1	1,843
"Clouded" wares, tortoiseshell, mottled glazed cream-colored ware	1755	1	1,755
North Devon gravel tempered ware	1713	2	3,426
Everted rim, undecorated tin-enameled ointment pot (delft)	1750	1	1,750
"Finger-painted" wares (polychrome slip on creamware or pearlware)	1805	8	14,440
Enameled hand-painted creamware	1788	5	8,940
Creamware	1791	111	198,801
Underglazed polychrome pearlware, directly stenciled	1830	6	10,980
Embossed pearlware	1810	1	1,810
Transfer-printed pearlware	1818	61	110,898
"Annular wares" pearlware	1805	13	23,465
Underglaze blue hand-painted pearlware	1800	2	3,600
Blue and green-edged pearlware	1805	7	12,635
Undecorated pearlware	1805	32	57,760
Total		355	637,371

Ceramic Formula Computation

637,288 ÷ 355 = 1795.2 x .87 = 1561.8 + 235.5 = 1797.3

TABLE 14
38B IV

Ceramic Type	Type Median	Sherd Count	Product
White salt-glazed stoneware	1763	4	7,052
"Black basaltes" stoneware	1785	1	1,785
Engine-turned unglazed red stoneware	1769	2	3,538
Lead-glazed slipware (combed yellow)	1733	1	1,733
Whiteware	1860	6	11,160
North Devon gravel-tempered ware	1713	1	1,713
"Finger-painted" wares (polychrome slip on creamware or pearlware)	1805	4	7,220
Creamware	1791	12	21,492
Transfer-printed creamware	1790	1	1,790
Transfer-printed pearlware	1818	6	10,908
"Annular wares" pearlware	1805	3	5,415
Blue and green-edged pearlware	1805	1	1,805
Undecorated pearlware	1805	10	18,050
Total		52	93,661

Ceramic Formula Computation

93,661 ÷ 52 = 1801.2 x .87 = 1567 + 235.5 = 1802.5

TABLE 15
38B IVa

Ceramic Type	Type Median	Sherd Count	Product
Overglaze enameled China trade porcelain	1808	14	25,312

162

TABLE 15, continued

Ceramic Type	Type Median	Sherd Count	Product
English porcelain	1770	5	8,850
British brown stoneware	1733	3	5,199
Westerwald, stamped blue floral devices, geometric designs	1738	1	1,738
Transfer-printed white salt-glazed stoneware	1760	1	1,760
White salt-glazed stoneware	1763	19	33,497
"Black basaltes" stoneware	1785	1	1,785
Engine-turned unglazed red stoneware	1769	2	3,538
Whiteware	1860	20	37,200
Mocha	1843	1	1,843
"Clouded" wares, tortoiseshell, mottled glazed cream-colored ware	1755	4	7,020
North Devon gravel-tempered ware	1713	1	1,713
Everted rim, undecorated tin-enameled ointment pot (delft)	1750	19	33,250
"Finger-painted" wares (polychrome slip on creamware or pearlware)	1805	9	16,245
"Annular wares" creamware	1798	1	1,798
Enameled hand-painted creamware	1788	2	3,576
Creamware	1791	62	111,042
Underglazed polychrome pearlware, directly stenciled	1830	2	3,660
Transfer-printed pearlware	1818	27	49,086
"Annular wares" pearlware	1805	10	18,050
Underglaze blue hand-painted pearlware	1800	2	3,600

TABLE 15, continued

Ceramic Type	Type Median	Sherd Count	Product
Undecorated pearlware	1805	16	28,880
Total		222	398,642

Ceramic Formula Computation

398,559 ÷ 222 = 1795.3 x .87 = 1561.9 + 235.5 = 1797.4

TABLE 16
38B V

Ceramic Type	Type Median	Sherd Count	Product
Overglaze enameled China trade porcelain	1808	5	9,040
English porcelain	1770	1	1,770
Westerwald, stamped blue floral devices, geometric designs	1738	1	1,738
Moulded white salt-glazed stoneware	1753	1	1,753
White salt-glazed stoneware	1763	8	14,104
White salt-glazed stoneware plates	1758	1	1,758
Engine-turned unglazed red stoneware	1769	1	1,769
Lead-glazed slipware (combed yellow)	1733	1	1,733
Whiteware	1860	12	22,320
"Clouded" wares, tortoiseshell, mottled glazed cream-colored ware	1755	1	1,755
"Finger-painted" wares (polychrome slip on creamware or pearlware)	1805	2	3,610
Creamware	1791	56	100,296
Transfer-printed pearlware	1818	20	36,360

164

TABLE 16, continued

Ceramic Type	Type Median	Sherd Count	Product
Underglaze polychrome pearlware	1805	3	5,415
"Annular wares" pearlware	1805	18	32,490
Underglaze blue hand-painted pearlware	1800	1	1,800
Blue and green-edged pearlware	1805	1	1,805
Undecorated pearlware	1805	17	30,685
Total		150	270,201

Ceramic Formula Computation

270,201 ÷ 150 = 1801.3 x .87 = 1567.2 + 235.5 = 1802.7

TABLE 17
38B Va

Ceramic Type	Type Median	Sherd Count	Product
Overglaze enameled China trade porcelain	1808	20	36,160
English porcelain	1770	1	1,770
British brown stoneware	1733	2	3,466
Westerwald, stamped blue floral devices, geometric designs	1738	2	3,476
White salt-glazed stoneware	1763	21	37,023
"Black basaltes" stoneware	1785	1	1,785
Engine-turned unglazed red stoneware	1769	1	1,769
Lead-glazed slipware (combed yellow)	1733	4	6,932
Whiteware	1860	22	40,920
Mocha	1843	1	1,843

TABLE 17, continued

Ceramic Type	Type Median	Sherd Count	Product
"Clouded" wares, tortoiseshell, mottled glazed cream-colored ware	1755	5	8,775
Refined agateware	1758	6	10,548
Pedestal-footed type ointment pot (delft)	1780	2	3,560
Everted rim, undecorated tin-enameled ointment pot (delft)	1750	2	3,500
Undecorated tin-enameled ware (delft), white	1720	3	5,160
"Finger-painted" wares (polychrome slip on creamware or pearlware)	1805	8	14,440
Creamware	1791	70	125,370
Transfer-printed pearlware	1818	13	23,634
"Annular wares" pearlware	1805	13	23,465
Blue and green-edged pearlware	1805	2	3,610
Undecorated pearlware	1805	28	50,540
Total		227	409,733

Ceramic Formula Computation

409,646 ÷ 226 = 1812.6 x .87 = 1576.9 + 235.5 = 1812.4

TABLE 18
38B VI

Ceramic Type	Type Median	Sherd Count	Product
Overglaze enameled China trade porcelain	1808	14	25,312
Nottingham stoneware	1755	1	1,755

TABLE 18, continued

Ceramic Type	Type Median	Sherd Count	Product
Moulded white salt-glazed stoneware	1753	3	5,259
White salt-glazed stoneware	1763	4	7,052
Mocha	1843	3	5,529
"Clouded" wares, tortoiseshell, mottled glazed cream-colored ware	1755	2	3,510
Refined agateware	1758	7	12,306
Creamware	1791	17	30,447
Transfer-printed pearlware	1818	3	5,454
"Annular wares" pearlware	1805	3	5,415
Undecorated pearlware	1805	7	12,635
Total		64	114,674

Ceramic Formula Computation

114,425 ÷ 64 = 1787.9 x .87 = 1555.5 + 235.5 = 1791

TABLE 19
38C

Ceramic Type	Type Median	Sherd Count	Product
Overglaze enameled China trade porcelain	1808	8	14,464
Moulded white salt-glazed stoneware	1753	1	1,753
White salt-glazed stoneware	1763	4	7,052
"Black basaltes" stoneware	1785	1	1,785
Engine-turned unglazed red stoneware	1769	50	88,450
Lead-glazed slipware (combed yellow)	1733	4	6,932

TABLE 19, continued

Ceramic Type	Type Median	Sherd Count	Product
Whiteware	1860	2	3,720
"Clouded" wares, tortoiseshell, mottled glazed cream-colored ware	1755	3	5,265
Refined agateware	1758	2	3,516
"Finger-painted" wares (polychrome slip on creamware or pearlware)	1805	5	9,025
Creamware	1791	31	55,521
Embossed pearlware	1810	1	1,810
Transfer-printed pearlware	1818	13	23,634
"Annular wares" pearlware	1805	7	12,635
Blue and green-edged pearlware	1805	1	1,805
Undecorated pearlware	1805	20	36,100
Total		153	273,467

Ceramic Formula Computation

273,467 ÷ 153 = 1787.4 x .87 = 1555 + 235.5 = 1790.5

TABLE 20
38D

Ceramic Type	Type Median	Sherd Count	Product
White salt-glazed stoneware	1763	1	1,763
Engine-turned unglazed red stoneware	1769	3	5,307
Lead-glazed slipware (combed yellow)	1733	1	1,733
Creamware	1791	7	12,537

168

TABLE 20, continued

Ceramic Type	Type Median	Sherd Count	Product
Underglaze polychrome pearlware, directly stenciled	1830	1	1,830
Transfer-printed pearlware	1818	4	7,272
Undecorated pearlware	1805	3	5,415
Total		20	35,857

Ceramic Formula Computation

35,857 ÷ 20 = 1792.8 x .87 = 1559.8 + 235.5 = 1795.3

TABLE 21
38H

Ceramic Type	Type Median	Sherd Count	Product
Overglaze enameled China trade porcelain	1808	11	19,888
Nottingham stoneware	1755	2	3,510
British brown stoneware	1733	1	1,733
Westerwald, stamped blue floral devices, geometric designs	1738	2	3,476
Moulded white salt-glazed stoneware	1753	2	3,506
White salt-glazed stoneware	1763	22	38,786
White salt-glazed stoneware plates	1758	5	8,790
"Black basaltes" stoneware	1785	1	1,785
Engine-turned unglazed red stoneware	1769	20	35,380
Lead-glazed slipware (combed yellow)	1733	12	20,796
Whiteware	1860	2	3,720

TABLE 21, continued

Ceramic Type	Type Median	Sherd Count	Product
Mocha	1843	6	11,058
"Clouded" wares, tortoiseshell, mottled glazed cream-colored ware	1755	2	3,510
Refined agateware	1758	6	10,548
Pedestal-footed type ointment pot (delft)	1780	1	1,780
Everted rim, undecorated tin-enameled ointment pot (delft)	1750	3	5,250
18th-century decorated tin-enameled ware (delft)	1750	4	7,000
"Finger-painted" wares (polychrome slip on creamware or pearlware)	1805	17	30,685
Enameled hand-painted creamware	1788	12	21,456
Creamware	1791	107	191,637
Underglazed polychrome pearlware, directly stenciled	1830	5	9,150
Embossed pearlware	1810	2	3,620
Transfer-printed pearlware	1818	41	74,538
"Annular wares" pearlware	1805	7	12,635
Underglaze blue hand-painted pearlware	1800	1	1,800
Blue and green-edged pearlware	1805	4	7,220
Undecorated pearlware	1805	62	111,910
Total		360	645,167

Ceramic Formula Computation

644,752 ÷ 360 = 1791 x .87 = 1558.1 + 235.5 = 1793.6

170

TABLE 22
38L

Ceramic Type	Type Median	Sherd Count	Product
Overglaze enameled China trade porcelain	1808	11	19,888
British brown stoneware	1733	1	1,733
White salt-glazed stoneware	1763	9	15,867
Lead-glazed slipware (combed yellow)	1733	3	5,199
Mocha	1843	4	7,372
"Clouded" wares, tortoiseshell,	1755	1	1,755
18th-century decorated tin-enameled ware (delft)	1750	5	8,750
"Finger-painted" wares (polychrome slip on creamware or pearlware)	1805	1	1,805
Enameled hand-painted creamware	1788	1	1,788
Creamware	1791	34	60,894
Transfer-printed creamware	1790	1	1,790
Underglaze polychrome pearlware, directly stenciled	1830	1	1,830
Transfer-printed pearlware	1818	13	23,634
"Annular wares" pearlware	1805	8	14,440
Blue and green-edged pearlware	1805	1	1,805
Undecorated pearlware	1805	6	10,830
Total		100	179,380

Ceramic Formula Computation

179,048 ÷ 100 = 1790.5 x .87 = 1557.7 + 235.5 = 1793.2

TABLE 23
38N

Ceramic Type	Type Median	Sherd Count	Product
Overglaze enameled China trade porcelain	1808	5	9,040
White salt-glazed stoneware	1763	2	3,526
Refined agateware	1758	1	1,758
18th-century decorated tin-enameled ware (delft)	1750	1	1,750
Undecorated white tin-enameled ware (delft)	1720	1	1,720
Creamware	1791	2	3,582
Total		12	21,376

Ceramic Formula Computation

21,376 ÷ 12 = 1781.3 x .87 = 1549.8 + 235.5 = 1785.3

APPENDIX E: PIPE STEM DATING

The pipe stem dating formula has been in use for many years and has certain
drawbacks, one of the most serious being the large-sized sample necessary
before representative dates can be determined. A second problem is that the
more recent the site or area being excavated, the less reliable the date obtained (Noel Hume 1972:298-301). The formula originally set forth by Harrington
(1954) was subsequently modified by Binford (1962), and although there have been
discussions of further modifications (see especially Historical Archaeology
Forum, Section Two in the Conference on Historic Site Archaeology Papers 1971),
the Binford formula was applied to the Drayton Hall collection. The formula
is as follows:

$$Y = 1931.85 - 38.26X$$

where Y is the mean date for the group, 1931.85 the theoretical date when the
pipe stem hole would disappear totally, 38.26 the number of years between each
1/64-inch decrease and X the mean stem hole diameter for the sample. The entire
formula is based on the observation that through time the stem hole diameters
of kaolin pipes decrease and on the postulation that they decrease at a constant rate.

Following are the calculations for dating the pipe stem collections in certain
areas of the Drayton Hall excavations. As can be seen when compared to the
mean ceramic dating formula and with known date brackets for areas of the site,
the dates obtained by using the pipe stem method are consistently earlier.

TABLE 1
Pipe Stem Dating

Hole Diameter	Fragments	Product
Units 10 and 11 (Trash Pit)		
7/64"	1	7
6/64"	13	78
5/64"	84	420
4/64"	17	68
Total	115	573 = 4.983

$Y = 1931.85 - 38.26(4.983) = 1743.20$
(mean ceramic date = 1790.3)

Exterior Occupation Level, South Flanker		
7/64"	0	0
6/64"	4	24
5/64"	14	70
4/64"	3	12
Total	21	106 = 5.048

$Y = 1931.85 - 38.26(5.048) = 1738.71$
(mean ceramic date = 1788.5)

174

TABLE 1 - Continued

Hole Diameter	Fragments	Product
	Interior Destruction Debris, South Flanker	
7/64"	2	14
6/64"	10	60
5/64"	9	45
4/64"	1	4
Total	22	123 = 5.591

Y = 1931.85 - 38.26(5.591) = 1717.94
(mean ceramic date = 1786.7)

	Exterior Destruction Debris, South Flanker	
7/64"	2	14
6/64"	6	36
5/64"	37	185
4/64"	9	36
Total	54	271 = 5.018

Y = 1931.85 - 38.26(5.018) = 1739.86
(mean ceramic date = 1790.4)

175

TABLE 1 - Continued

Hole Diameter	Fragments	Product
	Unit 38	
7/64"	1	7
6/64"	35	210
5/64"	94	470
4/64"	25	100
Total	155	787 = 5.077

Y = 1931.85 - 38.26(5.077) = 1737.6
(mean ceramic date = 1792.9)

APPENDIX F: CERAMICS ANALYSIS

The historic period ceramics are discussed based on the taxonomic system
developed by J. Jefferson Miller and Lyle M. Stone for ceramic analysis at
Fort Michilimackinac (1970). Alterations in the order of presentation have
been made in the Earthenware Class, some types have been eliminated if they
were absent and additions were made to include groups for pearlware, whiteware and a few additional types not found at the fort. It is not the
purpose of this report to present detailed discussion of these ceramic types
as such, and interested readers should consult the work of Miller and Stone
as well as Noel Hume's Colonial Artifacts (1972) for details. Detailed
information on the provenience of these ceramics can be found in Appendix G,
which is a separate volume to this report entitled Quantification of
Artifacts from the Drayton Hall Excavations, and is available in limited
quantity.

CLASS A: EARTHENWARE

Group I: Coarse Earthenware
(10.9 Percent of Historic Period Ceramics Recovered)

Coarse earthenware is here defined as low-fired, crude pottery with a
minimum of decoration, glazed or unglazed, that was used for kitchen purposes
for the most part. The kitchenware includes crocks, milk and cream pans,
jars, bowls and jugs.

Type A. Unglazed Redware. (Thick red body, unglazed or slip covered on the
interior surfaces; North America*; 18th and 19th centuries.) About one-
third of the recovered unglazed redware sherds were slip covered on the
interior. All the sherds were from utilitarian wares such as milk pans,
bowls or flower pots.

Type B. Brown-glazed Redware. (Red bodied, covered on one or both sides
with a brown lead glaze; England and North America; 18th and 19th centuries.)
There were 165 sherds of this type, again consisting of the utilitarian
wares, including milk pans and crocks.

Type C. Green-glazed Earthenware. (Low-fired body, covered with green
lead glaze; England and North America; 18th century.) The majority of
the sherds of this type were storage vessels. A number of the green-
glazed sherds were the heavily gravel-tempered North Devonshire wares
manufactured in England between 1680 and 1760 (Noel Hume 1972:133)
(fig. 54).

Type D. Yellow-glazed Earthenware. (Low-fired, body covered with a yellow
lead glaze; France, French Canada; first half 18th century.) Only two

---

*Location indicates place of manufacture.

Figure 54: North Devon-
shire gravel-tempered
earthenware, green lead-
glazed milk pans. Top
from Unit 11C (8-13/16"
maximum width); middle
from Unit 2F (4-19/32"
rim to base); bottom
from Unit 10B and 11C
(6-1/2" outside dia-
meter). Top and bottom
fragments are from the
same vessel.

sherds, from a storage vessel, were recovered. These are small fragments and are not of sufficient size to allow a definite attribution as French. Rather, they are probably of local origin.

Type E. Slip-decorated Earthenware. (Buff-colored body, covered with a white slip and decorated with brown slip lines or dots. Overall, a clear lead glaze; England; 18th century -- or red-bodied, decorated with white slip lines or dots, with occasional splashes of copper green, all covered by a clear lead glaze; North America; second half of 17th century to first half of 19th century, fig. 55). There were 384 sherds of slip-decorated earthenware, combed, trailed or dotted. There were a large number of sherds from the Bristol or Stafford-shire districts of England, mainly consisting of posset cups, small bowls and dishes. The North American wares bear a strong resemblance to those of Pennsylvania manufacture, although they could be of local origin as well. One unusual piece, covered with a brilliant green slip, is possibly of French origin (Noel Hume, personal communication).

Type F. Clear-glazed Earthenware. (Coarse red bodied, covered with a clear lead glaze; England and North America; 18th century.) A few sherds of this type were found, belonging to storage vessels.

Type G. Black Lead-glazed Earthenware. (Coarse red bodied, covered by a black lead glaze; probably North America; 18th century.) The recovered sherds of this ware represent small bowls or cups. Also recovered were six sherds of the coarse black lead-glazed storage vessels manufactured in the Buckley district of England.

Group II: Colono-Indian Wares
(14.9 Percent of Historic Period Ceramics Recovered)

These wares are discussed in detail in the section on trade artifacts (page 62).

Group III: Tin-Glazed Earthenware
(5.2 Percent of Historic Period Ceramics Recovered)

Although tin-glazed earthenware was manufactured throughout most of western Europe during the 18th century, all of the examples from Drayton Hall are of English or Dutch origin. Even though it was not possible to ascribe any sherds to other origins, it is feasible that some of the smaller fragments that have little or no decoration could have come from vessels of French manufacture. Tin-glazed earthenware is a soft paste earthenware covered by a lead glaze to which tin oxide has been added, thus creating an opaque whitish glaze.

Type A. Blue and White. (Includes plain white and white decorated with blue; England, France; 18th century.) All the sherds of this type were ascribed to England, although it is possible that some French faience is present but unidentified. The predominant vessel forms are ointment jars, wash basins or chamber pots, with only a few plates represented (fig. 56). Several sherds were recovered with no glaze at all, and the majority of the sherds were in very poor condition.

Figure 55: British slip-decorated earthenware.
Left, Staffordshire or Bristol ware posset cup.
Pale buff body, yellow glaze with brown dots and
combing, Units 10B, 11B and 17C. Middle, Staffordshire ware plate sherds, red body, yellow
glaze with brown dots and trailing, Units 17G
and 22B. (Sherd at left, 1-9/16" maximum width.)
Lower photo: probably American slip-decorated
earthenware. Dish (top), Unit 10B; shallow
bowl (bottom), 6 3/16" maximum width, Units 34B,
38B Va, 38C, 38J and 38Q.

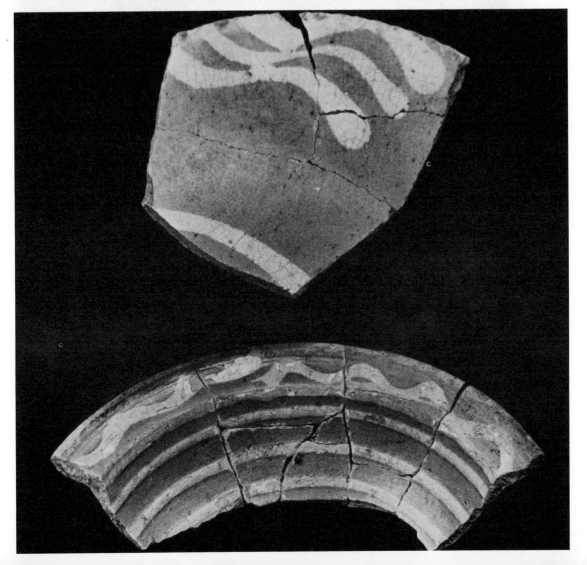

180

Figure 56: Tin-glazed earthenware ointment pot, Unit
38B IVa and 38H.

Type B. Polychrome. (Decorated in one or more colors, excluding plain blue
and white (Type A); England, France; 18th century.) Only seven polychrome tin-
glazed earthenware sherds were found, and these all appear to be English,
although the small size of these makes definite attribution difficult. All
these sherds were from ointment pots.

Type C. Brown and White. (White tin-glazed interior, brown lead-glazed
exterior; France; 18th century.) No sherds of this type were discovered.
This is surprising since this type is considered very common on American
sites of the Revolutionary War period (Noel Hume 1960:559-61) and also in
light of the fact that a high percentage of this type has been recovered
from the excavation of the American and British midden deposits at Fort
Moultrie (South 1974). It is quite possible that the lack of this ware
is a reflection of wealth, since it was considered an inferior ware.

Type D. Powdered Blue and Purple. (Decorated with powdered blue or powdered
purple grounds; England; last half 18th century.) Only six sherds, all purple,
of this type were recovered. The pieces were very small but appear to have
come from ointment pots.

Type E. Tile. (Blue and white or blue and white with powdered purple ground;
English, Dutch; late 16th century to present.) Of the almost 200 tile fragments
excavated, 60 percent were found in the area immediately outside the center side
door of the south facade of the main house. Several of the tiles have a
powdered purple border and most of the tiles are of Dutch origin. A family
tradition persists that the tiles for the upstairs fireplaces came from a
wrecked Dutch merchantship.

Numerous styles and patterns of tile are represented, including a lattice and
floral pattern in blue on white (fig.57) that appears on at least four tiles.
Other patterns include floral bouquets and fishing scenes. All the tiles are
5/16th-inch-thick or less and would have been used for fireplace lining or
wall skirting.

The limited role that tin-glazed earthenware seems to have played at Drayton
Hall is not surprising since this ware was being replaced by the 1740s
(Drayton Hall was not completed until 1742) by white salt-glazed stoneware.
The later tin-glazed earthenwares were confined largely to tiles and ointment
pots. The Drayton artifacts fit this pattern, but the total absence of the
brown and white Rouen faience so common during the Revolutionary War period
is curious. A reasonable explanation would be that the house was not lived
in until 1780 when Charles Drayton assumed occupancy. But the brown and
white Rouen faience was being imported through 1784 (Miller and Stone 1970:
38; Prime 1969:146) and was available in Charleston, as confirmed by its
presence at Fort Moultrie. This tends to confirm the idea that this ware
was not present for social and economic reasons, rather than lack of availability.

One fragment of what may have been an heirloom tin-glazed earthenware plate
was found during excavation of a ground-floor room (4B), a fragment of a
blue-dash charger, the only piece of such a vessel discovered. These large
flat plates were manufactured in England during the second half of the 17th
century; however, this fragment was found in a context dating from 1795 or
later, based on the presence of a blue transfer-printed pearlware fragment
and some lime-green bottle glass found at the same level.

182

Figure 57: Tin-glazed earthenware tile fragments, blue on white. Top, 5/8" across, from Unit 38B IVa; bottom left, Unit 22B; bottom right, Unit 17G.

Figure 58: Fine red-bodied earthenware, white slip band decorated with over-glaze red and yellow flow-ers; flowerpot and tray sherds. Top row, left to right: 1-1/32" across top, Unit 39A/AI; Unit 34B/FY, FZ and 38B Va/PD; Unit 39A/AL, AM. Bottom row, left to right: Unit 36B/AE, AF, AG, AH,AY; Unit 36B/AI, AJ, AL; Unit 35A/AI, AJ and 35D/BD.

Group IV: Fine Earthenware
(1.4 Percent of Historic Period Ceramics Recovered)

The fine earthenwares are distinguished from the coarse ones by being more
finely potted, closer grained, with more sophisticated decorative techniques.
The Whieldon-Wedgwood-type wares in particular gained great popularity during
the third quarter of the 18th century, and it is therefore curious to note
the singular lack of these types (the Whieldon-Wedgwood types alone consti-
tute only 0.5 percent of the total historic ceramic assemblage). There are
numerous colonial sites of this period that contain a far more representative
sample of this type of ware. It should be noted that the Whieldon-Wedgwood
wares date from the same period as the Rouen faience, which is also missing
from the Drayton Hall site. The following Whieldon-Wedgwood types consist
mainly of plate or tea service fragments.

Type A. Whieldon-Type Brown and Green Splash Glaze. (Cream-colored body with
a yellowish clear lead glaze interior and splashed brown and green lead glaze
on the exterior; England; 1740-75.) Only nine sherds of this type, all from
plates, were recovered.

Type B. Whieldon-Type Tortoiseshell Glaze. (Cream-colored body covered with
a mottled brown, cream, gray and green lead glaze; England; 1740-75.) Of the
small number of the Whieldon-Wedgwood types, this was the most common and in
one case is represented by several pieces of a spittoon.

Type C. Whieldon-Wedgwood Type Fruit and Vegetable Motifs. (Cream-colored body
molded in pineapple, cauliflower and cabbage relief patterns and decorated with
green, yellow and white lead glazes; England; 1740-75.) These very popular
wares are represented by only four sherds on the Drayton Hall site, two from
a pineapple motif vessel and two from a cauliflower motif vessel; all four
are from tea service pieces. The scarcity of this and the other types listed
leaves an interesting gap in the spectrum of Drayton Hall ceramics.

Type D. "Jackfield" Type. (Finely potted red to purple body covered by deep
black lead glaze, frequently oil-gilded in floral or foliate designs; England;
1745-90.) The Jackfield type wares are named for the town in which the ware
originated. It was subsequently copied by other potteries, including Wedgwood.
Forty-five sherds of this ware, all from tea services, were recovered at
Drayton Hall. None of the sherds had a recognizable oil-gilded design.

Type E. Refined Agateware. (Body of combined red and yellow clay covered with
clear lead glaze; England; 1740-75.) More than 25 sherds of this type were
recovered, the remains of a plate and a small dish.

Type F. Miscellaneous. (Probably English; 19th century.) There were 22 sherds
of a very finely turned, red-bodied earthenware recovered. This ware is
covered with a clear lead glaze, with a white slip band between the lip and
the shoulder on the exterior. Red and yellow overglaze flowers appear on the
white band. The sherds represent two vessels, which appear to be a small
flower pot tray and matching pot (fig. 58).

Group V: English Cream-Colored Earthenware
(22.8 Percent of Historic Period Ceramics Recovered)

Creamware was the most common ceramic type found on the site. This ware, which was perfected during the 1760s and reached its height of popularity during the prerevolutionary period, has a cream-colored earthenware body covered with a clear, yellowish lead glaze. Almost all creamware was manufactured in England, although a factory that produced this ware was established in Charleston in 1770 (Prime 1969:112). None of the creamware found was attributable to this source.

Type A. Undecorated. (No relief or painted decoration; England; 1762-1820.) Of the 2,443 creamware sherds, 2,209 were undecorated. This can be misleading, though, because most creamware vessels had relief-molded decoration confined to the rim, border or around handles and spouts, the rest of the body being plain. The most common forms found at Drayton Hall were dinner and soup plates, platters, serving dishes, tea wares and chamber pots. One pierced-work vegetable strainer was also recovered (fig. 59).

Type B. Relief Borders. (Decorated with various relief-molded borders; England; 1762-1820.) 99 relief borders of the following types were found (fig. 60): old feather edge (55), beaded edge (17), royal pattern (14), Queen's pattern (5), foliate (4), bead and gadroon (3) and shell edge (1, green) (Noel Hume 1972:222; Miller and Stone 1970:46). The vessel forms represented include plates, serving dishes and tea wares, but no chamber pots. From consideration of the ceramic assemblage, it seems that the single largest set of dishes at Drayton Hall was the old feather edge creamware, represented by 55 of the 99 edge fragments.

Type C. Polychrome. (Decorated over the glaze with polychrome enamel colors; England; 1765-1810.) Three polychrome creamware sherds, bearing a red bow linked by a black band border design, all from tea wares, were recovered (fig. 61).

Type D. Transfer-printed. (Decorated with black transfer-print over the glaze; England; 1765-1815.) Only two fragments of transfer-printed creamware were found, one showing a butterfly, the other too fragmentary for identification (fig. 61). Both were pieces from a tea service.

Type E. (a) Mocha, (b) finger-painted and (c) banded. (Decorated with (a) a brown fernlike ornament created from a mixture of tobacco juice and urine found in association with banded wares, (b) polychrome slip under the glaze, (c) horizontal bands of color under the glaze; England; 1780-1820.) Of the 26 sherds of this type, 14 were mocha, 3 finger-painted and 1 banded. It is not surprising that more of this type does not occur, because these are late designs that appear more frequently on pearlware, which was rapidly replacing creamware in popularity.

Handles, finials and spouts are decorative elements associated with plain or relief-molded creamware, and of the 15 pieces found, there were no spouts. The majority of the handles were plain, with either plain or foliate terminals. Several large flat handles derive from chamber pots.

Group VI: Pearlware
(21.3 Percent of Historic Period Ceramics Recovered)

Pearlware, the second most common ceramic type found at Drayton Hall, consists of a white body covered with a clear lead glaze to which some cobalt blue has

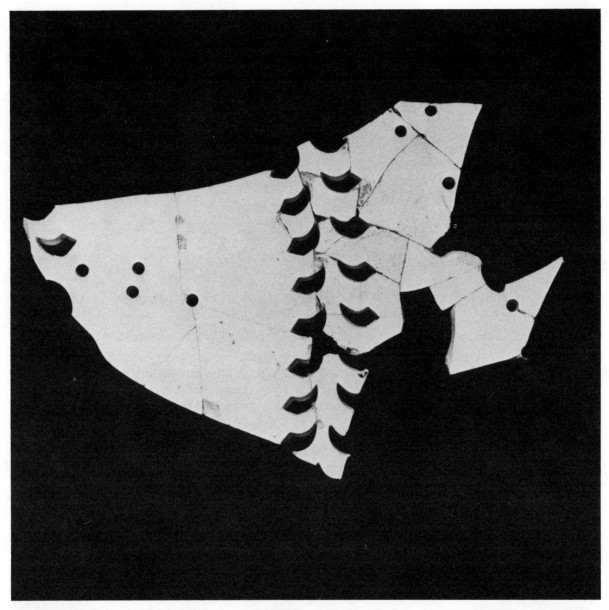

Figure 59: Creamware vegetable strainer (5-21/32" maximum height),
Unit 38B IVa.

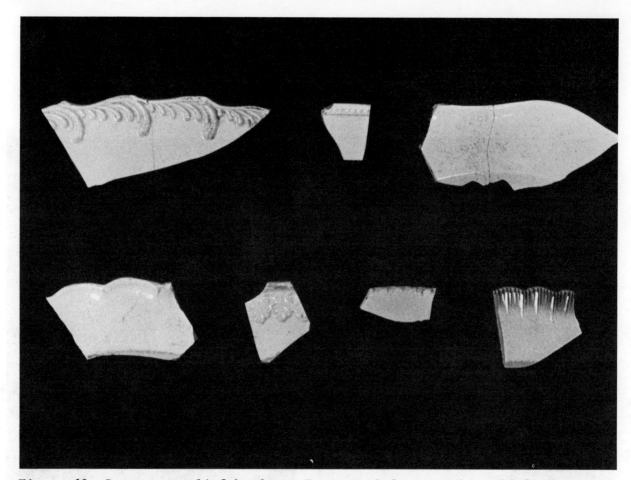

Figure 60: Creamware relief borders. Top row, left to right: old feather-edge plate (3-3/4" across), Unit 22B1 MB, MC; beaded edge plate, Unit 11C/VL; royal pattern plate, Unit 10B/WJ WY. Bottom row, left to right: Queen's pattern plate, Unit 38B Va/AA; raised loaf pattern plate, Unit 11B/KO; bead and gadroon plate edge, Unit 10B/WI; green shell edge, Unit 53/AH.

Figure 61: Creamware. Left, black transfer-printed butterfly, Unit 38L/CI; right, hand-painted polychrome, black and red, Unit 11B/LN.

been added, thus counteracting the inherent yellow cast in the lead glaze and producing a ware almost as white as the porcelains, but without the latter's translucency. In addition to plates, the pearlwares are most commonly found in the shape of bowls, mugs and jugs, often with annular decoration.

Type A. Undecorated. (No relief or painted decoration; England; 1780-1830.)
Pearlware sherds that come under this heading can be misleading since wares with only the rim or a small portion decorated can produce many undecorated fragments. The majority of undecorated sherds are from plates, bowls and chamber pots.

Type B. Transfer-printed. (Has transfer-printed designs in numerous motifs and colors under the glaze; England; 1795-1840.) All the transfer-printed pearlware found at Drayton Hall was blue, although pearlware was manufactured with other colors. One of the most popular patterns was the "willow" pattern, which is represented by about one-quarter of the transfer-printed sherds re-covered. Of all the transfer-printed wares, the vast majority were from plates, with several bowls and jars also represented. On the basis of the repeated patterns and the quantities of pearlware recovered, there was probably a set of these dishes in use at the plantation.

Type C. Shell Edge. (Has a molded shell-edge rim painted in blue, green, red or yellow; England; 1780-1830.) This decorative motif was quite popular, and the number of examples recovered at Drayton Hall indicates there probably were two sets of plates, one with a green edge, the other blue. The green-edge pieces were less common, about half the number as the blue, and were all from plates. The blue edge was mostly from plates, but a few sherds from bowls were recovered. (fig. 62). The quality of execution of these edge wares varied from very fine early wares to crude later ones, although there are some crude early examples as well as fine later examples. The Drayton collection shows this range fully. Several blue-edge sherds have embossed feather-like devices on the rims and these most likely date from after 1800. No red or yellow-edge sherds were found.

Type D. Hand-painted Blue and White. (Blue designs hand painted under the glaze; England; 1780-1820.) The most common designs used for blue hand painting were Chinese house patterns borrowed from the porcelains. A comparatively small number of these wares were found at Drayton Hall, the blue transfer-printed wares being more popular.

Type E. Hand-painted Polychrome. (decorated in hand-painted underglaze poly-chrome colors, usually in floral or geometric patterns; England; 1795-1840.)
This category can be divided in two, one category representing a pastel palette and popular from 1795 to 1815, the other using bright blue, orange, green and pinkish red colors directly stencilled onto the vessels, popular between 1820 and 1840. The Drayton Hall examples are largely from the former category, although several sherds of the later brighter hued wares are present. These wares are from tea bowls and tea services exclusively.

Type F. Annular Wares. (Decorated with horizontal bands of color, usually black, green, brown or blue, under the glaze, sometimes with additional decorative motifs; England; 1790-1820.) This was the second most common decorative motif on the Drayton Hall pearlwares found exclusively on bowls, mugs and jugs.

188

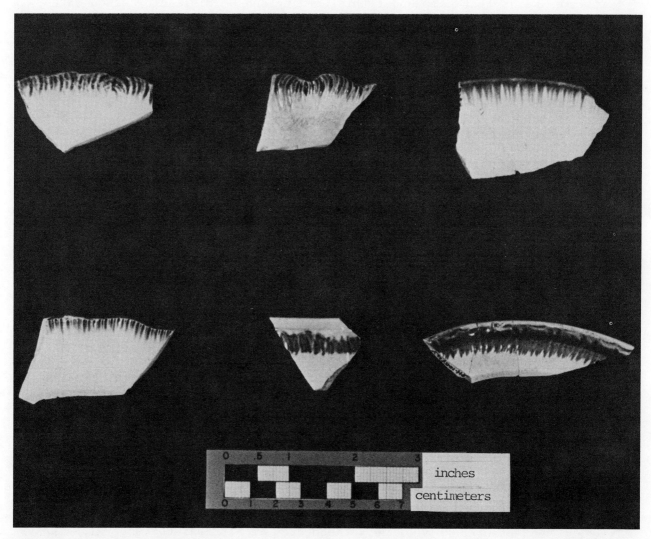

Figure 62: Blue, shell-edge pearlware. Top row, left to right: plates, Units 34B/DO, DM; 10B/UU; 18C/AY AX. Bottom row, left to right: plate, Unit 34B/DL, 38B IIIA/HL; bowl, Unit 38L; small dish, Unit 10B/CO, UY.

A subclass of the annular wares, but one that continued to be manufactured into the second half of the 19th century (1795-1890), is known as "mocha." This ware was produced by using a mixture of urine and tobacco juice to create brown fern-like decorations in banded zones on what was otherwise annular ware. Only 11 sherds with this motif were found at Drayton Hall in keeping with the general scarcity of wares dating from the last half of the 19th century.

Another motif found on banded wares known as "finger-painted" consists of cloud or worm-like swirling lines in blue, black, brown and white. These wares were most popular during the period 1790-1820, and along with those decorated by a similar technique known as "marbling," account for more than 100 of the 2,282 recovered pearlware sherds (fig. 63).

Finally, some annular wares had powdered blue and brown zones beneath the banding, but only two of these were found at Drayton Hall.

Group VII: Whiteware
(3.5 Percent of Historic Period Ceramics Recovered)

By the 1820s, pearlware was being replaced by the very hard whitewares and semiporcelains. These wares are difficult to date without the presence of factory marks and were manufactured from the 1820s into the 20th century. Perhaps the most noted variety was "Ironstone China" first manufactured by Mason in 1813. This thick, durable ware was quickly copied by other potteries and enjoyed great popularity.

Most of the patterns found on pearlware also appear on whiteware, with the exception of the finger painting and marbling techniques and the early pastel polychrome hand painting. The transfer-printed colors found at Drayton Hall were black, green and brown as well as blue (fig. 64). The use of transfer-print colors other than blue was introduced in the late 1820s (Shaw 1968:234-5). Only six "flow blue" sherds were found; flow blue was produced by adding extra cobalt blue to the clear lead glaze, causing the blue of the transfer-print to flow outside the edges of the pattern. Only 3.5 percent of all the ceramics found at Drayton Hall were whitewares, again pointing to limited occupation of the site from the last half of the 19th century to the present.

Group VIII: Yellow Ware
(0.3 Percent of Historic Period Ceramics Recovered)

During the last half of the 19th century and into the 20th century, the annular pearlwares were represented by a ware with a drab yellow body, with bands of light blue and raised white ridges, covered by a clear lead glaze. There were 28 sherds of this ware found at Drayton Hall.

CLASS B: STONEWARE

Stoneware is a highly fired, hard-bodied ceramic, which is slightly vitrified by the high firing temperature and, unlike the earthenwares, is impermeable to liquids. The addition of salt to the kiln during firing produces a clear, glassy, slightly rough surface. The benefits of using stoneware instead of the lead-glazed earthenwares were realized quite early. Stoneware is not only more durable but also less likely to cause lead poisoning. That there was contemporary awareness of the danger of lead poisoning is indicated by an article in the February 4, 1785, Pennsylvania Mercury quoted in Alfred Coxe Prime,

190

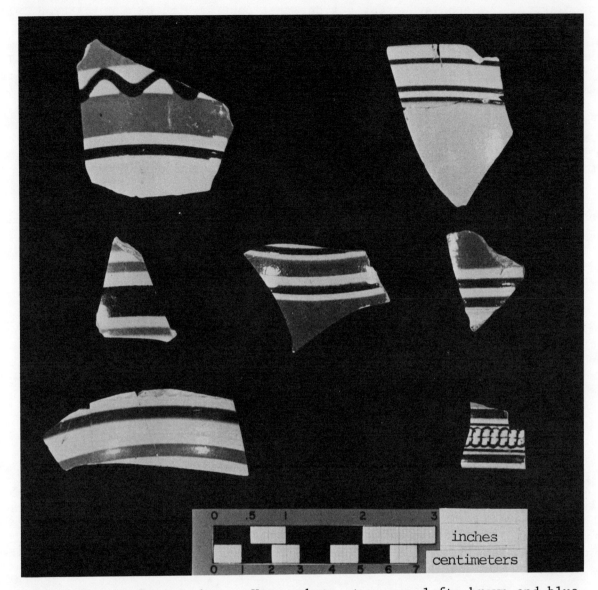

Figure 63: Annular pearlware. Upper photo, top row, left, brown and blue bowl, Unit 22B/YF; right, brown and yellow bowl, Unit 22B/CB, YR, ZG. Middle row, left to right: brown and blue bowls, Units 38B IIIA/AF, 38B V/AH, 38B VA/CK. Bottom row, left, brown and blue bowl with impressed band, Unit 38B V/AT, AV and 38B Va/CM; right, brown, black and blue mug base, Unit 23B/EH, EI. Opposite page, upper photo, left to right, blue, black, white, finger painted mug with green embossed rim, Unit 38B/IIa, 38B/IIIa, 38H; green and brown mug with handle, Unit 10A/GU, 10B/AUS; lower photo, green, brown, white and black finger painted mug with green embossed rim, Unit 38B/DN.

-Continued on next page

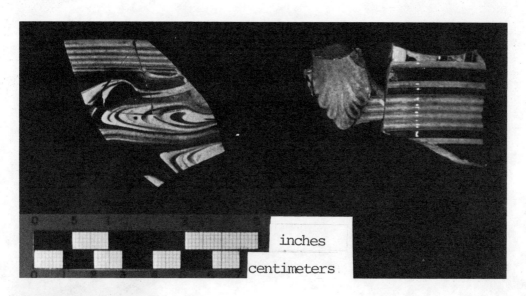

inches

centimeters

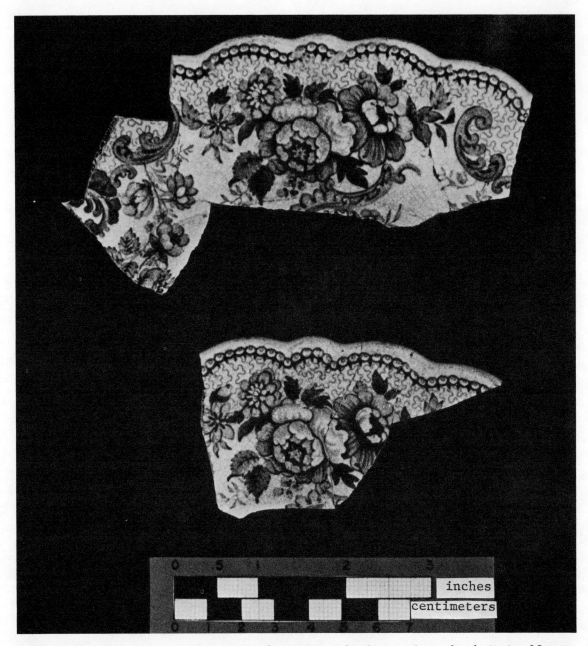

Figure 64: Whiteware, blue transfer-printed plate rims, both Unit 38B Va.

The Arts and Crafts in Philadelphia, Maryland and South Carolina, (1929)

Group I: English White Salt-glazed Stoneware
(4.5 Percent of Historic Period Ceramics Recovered)

One of the finest quality vessels, aside from the porcelains, recovered at
Drayton Hall was a white salt-glazed stoneware teapot. This type of stoneware was manufactured in England from the 1720s to the 1800s, but was at its
peak of popularity between 1740 and 1770; teapots, tankards, plates, bowls,
chamber pots and wash basins were all common vessel forms for this ware.

Type A. Undecorated. (White body covered with clear salt glaze with no relief
or painted decoration; England; 1720-1805.) The majority of white salt-glazed
stoneware recovered was without decoration of any sort. Of these plain sherds,
very few came from relief-decorated plates, but were from chamber pots or wash
basins. This is contrary to finds on other colonial sites, where most of the
white salt-glazed stoneware sherds represent pieces of dinner plates or other
pieces of dinner services (Miller and Stone 1970:70).

Type B. Relief Decorated. (White body, covered with a clear salt glaze and
decorated with molded relief patterns; England; 1740-70.) The majority of
relief-decorated sherds did not come from plates as would be expected (only
nine plate rims out of a total of 58 relief-decorated sherds were found)
but from teapots or tea service pieces. All the relief-molded plate rims were
of the "barley" pattern, but they were not identical(fig. 65).

One of the most elaborate vessels recovered from the entire site was the white
salt-glazed teapot with hunting scenes relief molded in panels (fig. 21), which
may have been manufactured at the pottery of Thomas and John Wedgwood. Several
fragments from another, similar teapot were also recovered.

Type C. Scratch Blue. (Grayish white body with incised decoration that was
filled with blue; covered with a clear salt glaze; England; 1740-70.)
Only two sherds of this ware, which was most popular during the third quarter
of the 18th century, were found (fig. 65). Both these pieces were from small
bowls, probably tea bowls. Although this ware was less common generally than
the plain or relief-decorated white salt-glazed stonewares, it is remarkable
for its scarcity at Drayton Hall.

Group II: Miscellaneous Stoneware
(5.5 Percent of Historic Period Ceramics Recovered.)

A wide variety of stoneware types come under this heading, ranging from the
highly prized, carefully executed "jasper ware" teapots of the late 18th
century to the coarse storage vessels manufactured throughout the eastern
United States from colonial times to the present.

Type A. Rhenish. (Gray with a clear salt glaze, decorated with incised,
molded, stamped or applied designs, with some pieces embellished with cobalt
blue under the glaze; Germany; 1700-75.) A few chamber pot fragments are among
the vessels represented by this ware, but the majority were mugs or tankards.
Comparatively little of this once popular ceramic type appeared on the site,
but this is possibly because similar, American-made wares were available at
the same time.

194

Figure 65: White, salt-glazed stoneware. Top row, left, barley pattern plate rim,
Unit 38H/GI, GJ; right, chamber pot handle base and finial, Unit 41B/AC, AD (3"
maximum height). Middle row, left to right: relief molded teapot body sherd, Unit
22C/BG; same, Unit 19L/EL; relief molded mug rim sherd, Unit 18F/AC and 19C/AH.
Bottom, scratch blue teaware body sherd, Unit 2A/BL.

Type B. Brown Stoneware. (Heavy bodied, decorated in brown colors and having a clear salt glaze; England and North America; 18th century.) The majority of sherds from this group were from large storage vessels. This ware was the most common of the coarse stonewares found at Drayton Hall. Although much of it is of British origin, including some examples of wares made in the Fulham and Lambeth districts of England, there are several sherds that appear to be of North American origin.

Also included among the brown stonewares are 23 sherds of Nottingham stoneware. This was a smooth brown stoneware with a shiny surface over a gray body. The fragments are incised in checkerboard squares and show the typical thin white line separating the glaze from the body (fig. 66). One sherd of Nottingham stoneware is covered on the exterior with small pieces of clay frit and is probably from some decorative vessel (Hillier 1968:111)

Type C. Miscellaneous Coarse Salt-glazed Stoneware. (Various body colors with salt glaze; England, North America; 18th and 19th centuries.) There were salt-glazed stoneware fragments of gray, gray with cobalt blue decoration, clear and red glazes; the most common was the gray salt glaze. These wares seem to consist of storage vessels and mugs and many are of local manufacture.

Type D. Fine Red Stoneware. (Unglazed, finely grained, red brown body; England; mid-18th century.) Less than half a dozen sherds of this type were recovered, three from one teapot with a stamped floral motif. The other sherds were also from tea wares (fig. 67).

Type E. Stoneware Bottles. (Light gray to buff body, with pale yellow slip from lip to midsection; American; last half 19th century.) A few bottle sherds from American-made products appear on the site and date from the mid 19th-century or later.

Type F. Black Stoneware. (Finely grained black body, either unglazed or with clear lead glaze on one or both sides; English; 1750-1820.) Thirty-five sherds of this very fine, engine-turned ware were found, one with a basket-weave design and another with a stamped decorative motif. These were all from tea wares (fig. 67).

Type G. Jasper-type Ware. Unglazed, finely grained stoneware in various colors, with sprigged decoration, often slip-decorated in contrasting color on the exterior; England; 1775-1825.) Five sherds of an oval, chocolate brown jasper-type ware teapot were found. The exterior is covered with a beige slip with chocolate brown sprigged design applied over the slip. This is one of the most decorative pieces found at Drayton Hall and probably dates from the last quarter of the 18th century (fig. 68).

Type H. Coarse Black Lead Glaze. (Coarse gray body covered by a heavy black lead glaze; North America [?]; 19th century [?].) Only 14 fragments of this ware were recovered, and it is possible that these may represent wares of local manufacture.

196

Figure 66: British brown stoneware. Top photo, left: Fulham-type storage jar mouth, (2-1/2" maximum height), Unit 10B/SS, ST and 10C/BZ; right, Fulham-type storage vessel body sherd, Unit 22B/GY. Lower photo, top row, left: Nottingham mug body sherd, Unit 22N/ACF (all Nottingham scale 1:4); right, Nottingham mug rim sherd, Unit 18B/CG. Bottom row, left, Nottingham mug handle sherd, Unit 22N/ACG; right, Nottingham with clay frit decoration, ornamental object, Unit 18C/BD.

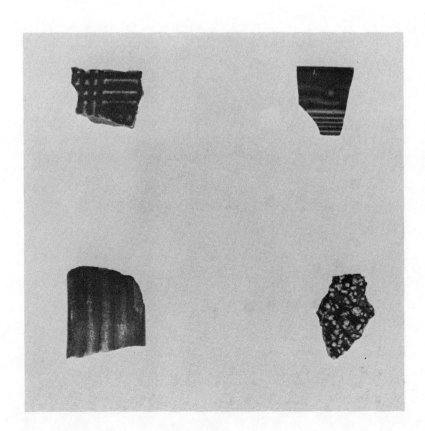

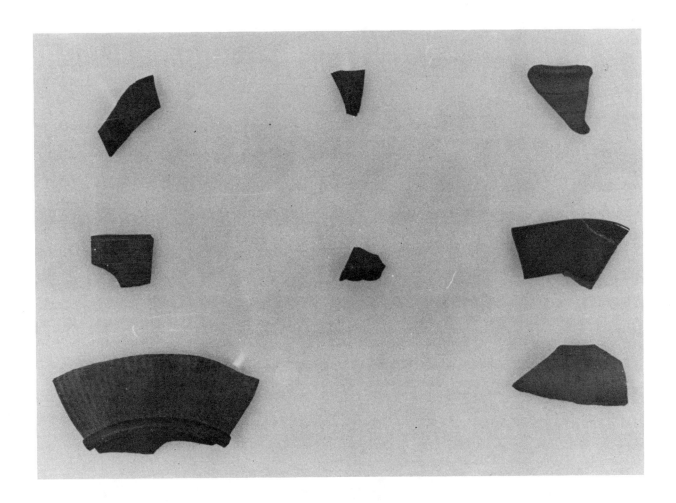

Figure 67: Top photo, black basalts. Top row, left to right: molded decoration, Unit 10B/TI; sprigged umbrella decoration, Unit 10B/AOZ; raised band, Unit 6A/AO; middle row: raised basket-weave design, Unit 2B/DB; raised gadroon, Unit 33B/EJ; clear lead glazed, Unit 10B/TJ, TK; bottom: raised ribs (2-5/16" maximum width); Unit 38B Va/MV; curved lip, Unit 17G/DA. Side photo, red dry-bodied stoneware. Top, sprigged flower decoration (1-1/16" maximum width), Unit 6B/BT; bottom left, same, Unit 6B/BS; right, molded fish-scale design, Unit 22B/IC.

198

Figure 68: Jasperware-type teapot base. Brown body, beige slip and brown sprigged decoration (1-15/16") maximum height), Unit 10B/UO.

Figure 69: Chinese export porcelain, blue underglaze, soft paste. Possibly provincial. Left, tea bowl interior and right, exterior, showing crazing and raised white slip decoration at the extreme right (scale 1:4), Unit 38B IVa/EA, EB, ML, QV.

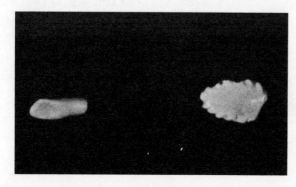

Figure 70: Undecorated Chinese export porcelain. Left, figurine hand, Unit 35G; right, leaf, Unit 38B V/BO (both actual size).

CLASS C: PORCELAIN

Porcelain is a highly fired, vitrified, more or less translucent ceramic made
from a combination of two clays: kaolin and petuntse, the first a feldspar and
the second a fusible feldspathic rock. It was first made by the Chinese,
probably during the T'ang Dynasty (A.D. 618-907). Porcelain was highly valued
and many 18th-century ceramic innovations in Europe were attempts to more
closely imitate Chinese porcelain.

Group I: Chinese Export Porcelain
(9.7 Percent of Historic Period Ceramics Recovered)

Porcelain was not directly imported from China into America until after the
Revolution. Until then it came by way of Europe because of the British im-
portation laws imposed during the 18th century. Despite the manufacture and
availability of European porcelains, Chinese export porcelain is dominant on
American sites dating from the 18th and early 19th centuries. In the 19th
century, as the Chinese export porcelain became more widely available and
less costly, it also began to deteriorate in quality.

In general, the quality of all porcelains recovered from the Drayton Hall
excavations was particularly fine and they were early in date. In addition,
there were several pieces of uncertain origin. A tea bowl decorated in white
slip under a glaze that when fired resembles water-marked paper (fig. 69),
represented an elaborate, uncommon type of porcelain. On the interior there
is a blue underglaze rim border, and there is noticeable crazing on the exterior. It seems likely that the three pieces of this ware are examples of
Chinese soft-paste porcelain.

Type A. Undecorated. (White hard paste, without relief molding or painted
decoration; China; 18th and 19th centuries.) A number of undecorated porcelain
sherds were found, the majority of which probably belong to decorated pieces.
The only possibly purely decorative ceramic items found were of plain porcelain,
one the hand from a figurine and the other a small leaf (fig. 70).

Type B. Blue and White. (White, hard paste, decorated in underglaze blue;
China; 18th through first half of 19th century.) The majority of the blue and
white porcelain found at Drayton Hall is of good quality and dates from the
18th century. These sherds represent tea services and plates (figs. 71,
72,73). There are only a few later, lower quality pieces.

Type C. Polychrome. (White to grayish white hard paste, decorated with enamel
colors over the glaze, often in conjunction with blue underglaze decoration;
China; 18th and 19th centuries.) In contrast to findings at other colonial
sites, there was substantially more overglaze enameled porcelain than plain blue
and white and more than the undecorated (i.e., 409 polychrome sherds vs. 276
plain blue and white ones). The overglaze polychrome porcelains were the most
costly to produce and the most prized. In this regard, the porcelain found on
an archaeological site seems to be the most positive indicator of wealth among
the ceramic artifacts (Stone 1970:88; Herman, Sands and Schecter 1974:66).

Several sherds of the polychrome wares were also decorated with a brown underglaze band on the lips of the vessels, a decorative motif found on porcelains
from the second and third quarters of the 18th century. A few identifiable
pieces of the "famille rose" and "famille verte" palettes were found (fig. 74).

200

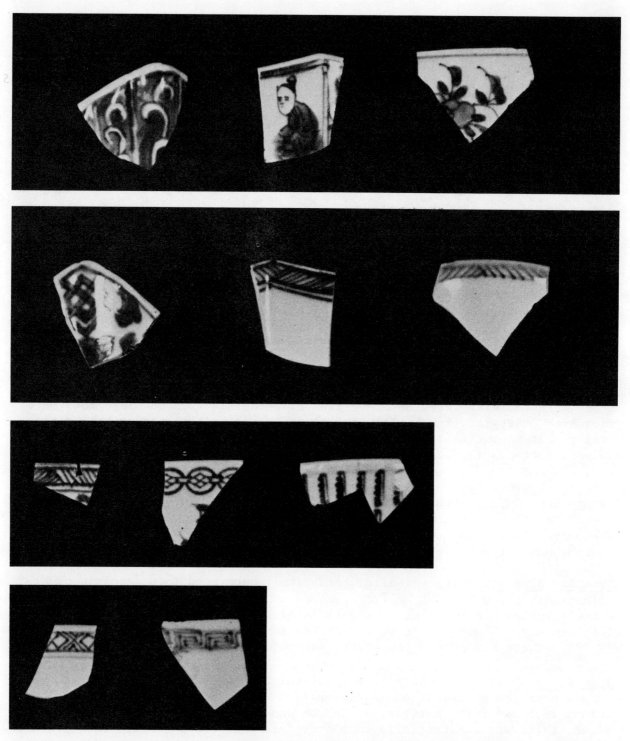

Figure 71: Chinese export porcelain rim sherds with blue underglaze. Left to right: exterior (top row) and interior (below) of sauce boat spout (actual size), Unit 37B/BY; exterior and interior of tea bowl rim (actual size), Unit 38J/AG; same, Unit 2F/DO. Third row: left to right: exterior tea bowl rim, Unit 10B/UL; same, Units 22B/AER and 33B/EY, EZ (1-3/16" across rim). Fourth row, interior of tea bowl rim, Unit 38B Va/EG; interior of tea bowl rim, Unit 35B/DE.

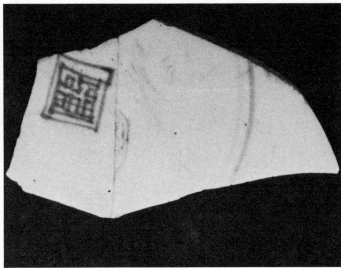

Figure 72: Chinese export porcelain platter (?), blue underglaze, molded.
Top, left, interior; right, exterior showing unidentified mark. Bottom,
detail of interior showing molded chrysanthemum design (3" maximum length),
Unit 7B/AL AM.

202

Figure 73: Chinese export porcelain, blue underglaze. Left, saucer (2-5/8"
along left edge); right, plate (2-7/8" along left edge), Unit 18C/AA.

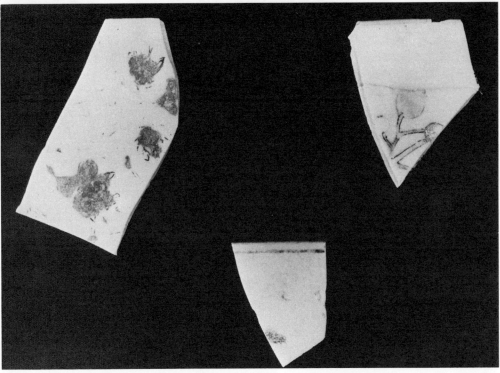

Figure 74: Chinese export porcelain, overglaze enameled. Top row, left, plate sherd, butterfly motif, famille verte, Unit 38B Va/EV; right, plate sherd, floral motif, famille rose, Unit 9D/AC. Bottom row, left, tea bowl rim, famille rose, Unit 22B/AFH; right, saucer sherd, floral motif, famille verte, Unit 2N/AU. Lower photo, left, plate sherd, floral motif, famille rose, Unit 11C/RN; right, bowl rim sherd, floral motif, famille verte, Unit 34B/MC, MD; center, bowl rim, floral motif, famille rose. (All scale 1:4)

The overall quality of these polychrome wares is generally high, and the majority date from the second and third quarters of the 18th century. Plates and tea wares were the most common vessel forms.

Type D. Brown Glaze. (Hard paste, blue and white interior decoration and an overall brown-glazed exterior; China; 18th century.) Only 10 sherds of this "dead leaf" ware, all from tea bowls, were found at Drayton Hall. This technique of decoration was most common during the period between 1740 and 1780.

Group II: English Porcelain
(0.2 Percent of Historic Period Ceramics Recovered)

On the basis of paste hardness, decorative motif and an ultraviolet light test, 20 sherds of the total artifact assemblage have been identified as English porcelain. English porcelain is frequently a soft-paste variety, which contains such ingredients as ground glass or bone ash in addition to the clays. It is vitrified and translucent but not as hard as hard-paste porcelain. Soft-paste porcelain shows a granular surface when fractured rather than the conchoidal fracture of hard-paste porcelain, and soft-paste porcelain emits a yellow light when viewed under ultraviolet light. Chinese porcelain emits purple light.

Of the English soft-paste porcelain recovered, one sherd is a handle finial, possibly manufactured by the Bow or Chelsea potteries, and another is a blue transfer-printed piece of the same origin.

Another piece of blue and white transfer-printed soft paste porcelain seems to originate from the Worcester or Caughley factories. There were four pieces with solid blue ground (fig. 68), all composing part of a spout from a teapot, and nine pieces of plain white soft-paste porcelain with stippled surfaces. (Arlene Palmer, personal communication).

Bail   small arched handle used as a drawer pull

Balk or baulk   strip of earth between the trenches of an excavation

Beaded board ceiling   consists of boards with a bead or semicircular molding at one edge

Blue-dash charger   large dish with decorated center and blue dashes around rim

Brickbat   piece of brick with one undamaged end

Builder's trench   trench in which foundations of a building are laid

Came   slender grooved lead piece used to hold panes of glass together

Chert   rock resembling flint, consisting essentially of cryptocrystalline quartz or fibrous chalcedony

Crazing   minute cracks or fissures in a network on the surface or glaze of plaster, cement, concrete or paint film; caused by shrinkage

Courses   parallel layers of bricks, stone, blocks, etc., usually horizontal, including any mortar laid with them

Escutcheon   protective or ornamental shield surrounding a key hole, light switch, etc.

Flankers   structures placed to the sides of a building, also called dependencies or pavilions

Grommet   eyelet of firm material to strengthen or protect an opening or to insulate or protect something passed through it

Ha-ha   ornamental ditch or sunken fence

Imbricated	overlapping in a regular order
Lees	settlings or dregs of liquor during fermentation and aging
Lensing	deposition of earth in lens-shaped layers
Lenticular deposition	lens-shaped deposit of earth
Marl	loose or crumbling earthy deposit (as of sand, silt or clay) that contains a substantial amount of calcium carbonate
Mean ceramic dating formula	formula applied to a collection of ceramic fragments to obtain a mean date for that collection
Metal	metal is used to describe glass in its vitreous state; while glass is used to define the products e.g., drinking glass, bottle glass, wine glass, etc.
Occupational level	stratigraphic level that contains debris deposited during the occupation of a site
Palette	colors put on a board (palette) for mixing
Pintle	pin of a hinge for a door or shutter
Posset cup	used for a hot drink of sweetened and spiced milk curdled with wine or ale
Provenience	source of origin
Provenience control number	number assigned to each level or feature of an excavation, used to provide control of the recovered data
Rim-fire	in reference to firearms, a cartridge that is fired by striking the rim, as opposed to a cartridge fired by striking the center
Reverberatory	furnace or kiln in which heat is radiated from the roof onto the material treated
Robbing (out)	taking out for reuse

Root mold	cavity left by decayed roots, which becomes filled with a mixture of the decayed material and the surrounding soil; distinguishable from the surrounding area by color and texture
Sherd	fragment of pottery vessel
Slip	mixture of fine clay and water that can be used both to cover and to decorate a vessel; applied before firing
Spline	long, thin strip of wood or metal that is inserted in a slot formed by two members, each of which is grooved and butted against the other
Stamped decoration	ornamentation of the soft clay of a pot by repeatedly impressing a design (checks or straight or curving lines) previously carved on a bone or wooden tool
Surface collected	picked up from the surface
Tang	narrow projection from the base of a tool or weapon blade to secure it to its shaft
Terminus ante quem	a time period not earlier than a certain date
Terminus post quem	a time period not later than a certain date
Terret	one of the rings on top of a harness pad through which the reins pass
Young-head	the first of two coinage portraits during the reign of a king (or queen), dividing the coins into those with "young" and "old" heads

NOTE: The following source materials were used in compiling this glossary:

Bray, Warwick, and Trump, David.
   1970   The American Heritage Guide to Archaeology. American Heritage Press, New York

Fleming, John, Honour, Hugh and Pevsner, Nikolaus.
   1976   The Penguin Dictionary of Architecture. Penguin Books, Middlesex, England

208

Harris, Cyril M., ed.
    1975   <u>Dictionary of Architecture and Construction</u>. McGraw-Hill Book Co.,
            New York

Noel Hume, Ivor.
    1969   <u>Historical Archaeology</u>. Alfred A. Knopf, New York

    1972   <u>A Guide to Artifacts of Colonial America</u>. Alfred A. Knopf, New York

    1976   "Glass in Colonial Williamsburg's Archaeological Collections."
            <u>Colonial Williamsburg Archaeological Series No. 1</u>. 2nd Printing.
            Colonial Williamsburg, Williamsburg, Va.

<u>Webster's Third New International Dictionary</u>.
    1971   G. and C. Merriam Co., Springfield, Mass.

BIBLIOGRAPHY

PRIMARY SOURCES

Charleston County, S.C., Courthouse
   n.d. Inventories and Wills. Books F, N, V, 2G, 3C, 3D, 3H, 4F, 4G,
         6W, 6Y, 9M, 10W, 12P, 12W.

   1687-1775 Inventories, Wills and Miscellaneous Papers. Volumes 52, 58, 60,
         62A, 65, 66, 69A, 69B, 72A, 75A, 75B, 80B, 82A, 83B, 85B, 86A, 90, 91A,
         91B, 95.

   1884 Plat Book. B 124 (August 20).

   1722-1862 Wills. Volumes 1, 3, 5, 9, 16, 23, 33, 34, 35, 37, 39, 42, 46, 47,
         49.

   1840-1927 Wills. Books, L, M, O, P, R, T, Y, BB.

Historic Charleston Foundation
   1779-1820 Diaries of Charles Henry Drayton, Sr.

Library of Congress, Manuscripts Division
   1732-1811 Laurens, Henry, Papers 0215-0919 M.

   1861-65 Manigault, Louis, Journal (1/200) 66-1439.

   1730-1805 Moultrie, William, Collection (1/2) MMC.

South Carolina State Archives, Columbia

        Cornwallis Papers. PRO 30/11/4, PRO 30/11/7.

   1790 First Census of the United States. (Heads of Families, South
         Carolina).

        Land Grants before 1776. Volumes 10 and 11.

        Memorials of Land Titles (Duplicate Series 1674-1776). Volume 1.

        Miscellaneous Records, 5 Letter Series. Volume 5M.

        Miscellaneous Records and Bills of Sale. Volumes FF, YY.

        Mortgages. Volume 32.

        Royal Grants. Volume 10 and Volume 11, Part 1.

        State Grants. Volumes 2 and 14.

SECONDARY SOURCES

History and Architecture

Andrews, Wayne
  1964 A Social History of American Architecture: Architecture, Ambition
        and Americans. The Free Press, New York.

Antiques
  1970 Charleston issue. April.

Architect's Emergency Committee
  1933 Great Georgian Houses in America. Volume I. Kalkhoff Press, New
        York. Reprinted by Dover Publications, New York, 1970.

  1937 Great Georgian Houses in America. Volume II. Scribner Press, New
        York. Reprinted by Dover Publications, New York, 1970.

Boorstin, Daniel J.
  1958 The Americans: The Colonial Experience. Vintage Books, New York.

Chamberlain, Samuel, and Chamberlain, Narcissa
  1956 Southern Interior of Charleston, South Carolina. Hastings House,
        New York.

Crane, Edward A., and Soderholtz, E. E.
  n.d. Examples of Colonial Architecture in South Carolina and Georgia.
        Bruno Hessling, Berlin.

Curtis, Elizabeth Gibbon
  1926 Gateways and Doorways of Charleston in the 18th and 19th Centuries.
        The Architectural Publishing Co., New York.

Drayton, John
  1802 A View of South Carolina, as Respects Her Natural and Civil
        Concerns. W.P. Young, Charleston. Reprinted by The Reprint Company,
        Spartanburg, S.C., 1972.

Dunbar, Carl O.
  1966 Historical Geology. 2nd ed. John Wiley and Sons, New York

Gipson, Lawrence Henry
  1962 The Coming of the Revolution. Harper and Row, New York.

Hamlin, Talbot
  1944 Greek Revival Architecture in America. Oxford University Press,
        New York.

Kent, William
  1727 Designs of Inigo Jones (privately printed).

Kimball, Fiske
  1922 Domestic Architecture of the American Colonies and of the Early
        Republic. Charles Scribner's Sons. Reprinted by Dover Publications,
        New York, 1966.

Leiding, Harriette K.
   1921 Historic Houses of South Carolina. J. B. Lippincott Company,
         Philadelphia.

Meriwether, Margaret Babcock, ed.
   1943 The Carolinian Florist of Governor John Drayton of South Carolina
         1766-1822. The South Caroliniana Library of the University of
         South Carolina, Columbia, S.C.

Montgomery, Charles, and Kane, Patricia E., eds.
   1976 American Art: 1750-1800 Towards Independence. The New York Graphic
         Society, Boston.

Morrison, Hugh Sinclair
   1952 Early American Architecture. Oxford University Press, New York.

Olmsted, Frederick Law
   1861 The Cotton Kingdom: A Traveler's Observations on Cotton and Slavery
         in the American Slave States. Mason Bros., New York. Reprinted by
         Alfred A. Knopf, New York, 1953.

Pennington, Patience
   1928 A Woman Rice Planter. The Macmillan Company, New York

Phillips, P. Lee
   1901 A List of Maps of America in the Library of Congress. Government
         Printing Office, Washington, D.C.

Pringle, Elizabeth W. Alston
   1940 Chronicles of Chicora Wood. Christopher Publishing House, Boston.

Providence Journal
   1885 "Drayton Hall and Magnolia Garden: A South Carolina Floral Paradise."
         Saturday, April 4.

Ravenel, Mrs. St. Julien (Harriott Horry Rutledge)
   1931 Charleston, the Place and the People. The Macmillan Company,
         New York.

Rogers, George C., Jr.
   1969 Charleston in the Age of the Pinckneys. University of Oklahoma Press,
         Norman, Okla.

Sarles, Frank B., Jr., and Shedd, Charles E.
   1964 Colonials and Patriots: Historic Places Commemorating Our Forebears,
         1700-1783. U.S. Department of the Interior, National Park Service,
         Washington, D.C.

Simons, Albert, and Lapham, Samuel, Jr.
   1927 Early Architecture of Charleston. Press of the American Institute of
         Architects, New York. Reprinted by the University of South Carolina,
         Columbia, S.C., 1970.

Smith, Alice R. Huger, and Smith, D. E. Huger
   1907 The Dwelling Houses of Charleston. J. B. Lippincott, New York.

212

Smith, Henry A. M.
   1919 "The Ashley River: Its Seats and Settlements." The South Carolina
        Historical and Genealogical Magazine 20(2):75-122.

Stoney, Samuel Gaillard
   1955 Plantations of the Carolina Low Country. rev. ed.   The Carolina Art
        Association, Charleston, S.C.

Taylor, George Rogers
   1951 The Transportation Revolution, 1815-1860. Volume 4: The Economic
        History of the United States. Holt, Rinehart and Winston, New York.

Ware, William Rotch
   1923 The Georgian Period, Being Photographs and Measured Drawings of
        Colonial Work with Text. 6 volumes U.P.C. Book Company, New York.

Wertenbaker, Thomas J.
   1949 The Golden Age of Colonial Culture. Cornell University Press,
        Ithaca and London.

Wilson, Everett B.
   1964 America, East: Its Architecture and Decoration. A. S. Barnes and
        Company, New York.

Wood, Peter H.
   1974 Black Majority: Negroes in Colonial South Carolina from 1670 through
        the Stono Rebellion. Alfred A. Knopf, New York.

Woolson, Constance Fenemore
   1875 "Up the Ashley and Cooper." Harper's New Monthly Magazine. December.

Archaeology

Ascher, Robert, and Fairbanks, Charles H.
   1971 "Excavation of a Slave Cabin: Georgia, U.S.A." Historical Archaeology
        5:3-17.

Baker, Steven G.
   1972 "Colono-Indian Pottery from Cambridge, South Carolina, with comments
        on the Historic Catawba Pottery Trade." The Notebook 4:3-30.

Beurdeley, Cecile, and Beurdeley, Michel
   n.d. A Connoisseur's Guide to Chinese Ceramics. Translated by Katherine
        Watson. Harper and Row, New York.

Binford, Lewis R.
   1962 "A New Method of Calculating Dates from Kaolin Pipe Stem Samples."
        Southeastern Archaeological Conference Newsletter 9:19-21.

Carrillo, Richard F.
   1974 "English Wine Bottles as Revealed by a Statistical Study: A Further
        Approach to Evolution and Horizon in Historical Archaeology."
        Conference on Historic Site Archaeology Papers, 1972, 7:290-317.

Deetz, James
1967 Invitation to Archaeology. The Natural History Press, Garden City,
      New York.

DuBoulay, Anthony
1973 Chinese Porcelain. Octopus Books, London.

Fairbanks, Charles H.
1956 "The Excavation of The Hawkins-Davison Houses, Frederica National
      Monument, St. Simon's Island, Georgia," The Georgia Historical
      Quarterly 40(September):213-29.

Garner, Sir Harry
1965 Oriental Blue and White. Thomas Yoseloff, New York
      New York.

Gill, Bruce Cooper
1976 "Ceramics in Philadelphia, 1780-1800: An Indicator of Socio-economic
      Status in a Major City of the New Nation." M.A. thesis, George
      Washington University.

Godden, Geoffrey, FRSA
1965 An Illustrated Encyclopedia of British Pottery and Porcelain.
      Bonanza Books, New York.

Harrington, J. C.
1954 "Dating Stem Fragments of Seventeenth and Eighteenth Century Clay
      Tobacco Pipes." Quarterly Bulletin of the Archaeological Society of
      Virginia 1:10-14.

Herman, Lynne L.; Sands, John O.; and Schecter, Daniel
1975 "Ceramics in St. Mary's County, Maryland During the 1840's: A
      Socioeconomic Study." The Conference on Historic Site Archaeology
      Papers, 1973. 8:52-93.

Hillier, Bevis
1968 Pottery and Porcelain 1700-1914: England, Europe and North America.
      Meredith Press, New York.

Honerkamp, Nicholas
1975 "The Material Culture of Fort Frederica: The Thomas Hird Lot." M.A.
      thesis, University of Florida.

Honey, W. B.
1964 English Pottery and Porcelain. Adam and Charles Black, London.

Huggins, Phillip Kenneth
1971 The South Carolina Dispensary, A Bottle Collector's Atlas and History
      of the System. Sandlapper Press, Columbia, S.C.

Jenyns, Soame
1965 Later Chinese Porcelain. Thomas Yoseloff, New York.

Kelso, William M.
  1974 "Captain Jones' Wormslow: A Historical, Archaeological, and Architec-
        tural Study of An Eighteenth-Century Plantation Site." Ph.D. disser-
        tation, Emory University.

Kidd, Kenneth E., and Kidd, Martha Ann
  1974 "A Classification System for Glass Beads for the Use of Field
        Archaeologists." Canadian Historic Sites 1:46-89.

LeCorbeiller, Clare
  1974 China Trade Porcelain: Patterns of Exchange, Metropolitan Museum of
        Art, New York.

Lee, Sherman E.
  n.d. A History of Far Eastern Art. Prentice-Hall and Harry N. Abrams,
        Englewood Cliffs, N.J., and New York.

McFarlane, Suzanne S.
  1975 "The Ethnohistory of a Slave Community: The Couper Plantation Site."
        M.A. thesis, University of Florida.

Miller, George L.
  1974 "A Tenant Farmer's Tableware: Nineteenth-Century Ceramics from Tabb's
        Purchase." Maryland Historical Magazine 69(December):197-210.

Miller, J. Jefferson, II, and Stone, Lyle M.
  1970 Eighteenth-Century Ceramics from Fort Michilimackinac: A Study in
        Historical Archaeology. Smithsonian Institution Press, Washington, D.C.

Mountford, Arnold R.
  1973 "Staffordshire Salt-Glazed Stoneware." Ceramics in America. Ian M.G.
        Quimby, ed. The University Press of Virginia, Charlottesville, Va.

Mudge, Jean M.
  1963 Chinese Export Porcelain for the American Trade, 1785-1835.
        University of Delaware Press, Newark, Del.

Neave-Hill, W.B.R.
  1976 Chinese Ceramics. St. Martin's Press, New York.

Noel Hume, Ivor
  1960 "Rouen Faience in Eighteenth-Century America." Antiques. 78:559-561.

  1962 "Excavations at Rosewell, Gloucester County, Virginia, 1957-1959."
        Contributions from the Museum of History and Technology, Paper 18.
        Smithsonian Institution, Washington, D.C.

  1963 Here Lies Virginia: An Archaeologist's View of Colonial Life and
        History. Alfred A. Knopf, New York.

  1966 "Excavations at Clay Bank in Gloucester County, Virginia, 1962-1963."
        Contributions from the Museum of History and Technology, Paper 52.
        Smithsonian Institution, Washington, D.C.

215

1966   "Excavations at Tutter's Neck in James City County, Virginia, 1960-1961."
       Contributions from the Museum of History and Technology, Paper 53.
       Smithsonian Institution, Washington, D.C.

1969   Historical Archaeology. Alfred A. Knopf, New York.

1969   "Glass in Colonial Williamsburg's Archaeological Collections."
       Colonial Williamsburg Archaeological Series No. 1. Colonial
       Williamsburg, Williamsburg, Va.

1969   "Pottery and Porcelain in Colonial Williamsburg's Archaeological
       Collections." Colonial Williamsburg Archaeological Series No. 2.
       Colonial Williamsburg, Williamsburg, Va.

1972   Guide to Artifacts of Colonial America. Alfred A. Knopf, New York.

1973   "Creamware to Pearlware: A Williamsburg Perspective." Ceramics in
       America. Ian M. G. Quimby, ed. The University Press of Virginia,
       Charlottesville, Va.

1974   "Digging for Carter's Grove." Colonial Williamsburg Archaeological
       Series No. 8. Colonial Williamsburg, Williamsburg, Va.

Olsen, Stanley J.
  1973   "Mammal Remains from Archaeological Sites, Part I. Southeastern and
         Southwestern United States." Papers of the Peabody Museum of Archaeology
         and Ethnology, Harvard University. Volume 1, No. 1. The Peabody Museum,
         Cambridge, Mass.

Otto, Hohn Solomon
  1975   "Status Differences and the Archeological Record: A Comparison of
         Planter, Overseer, and Slave Sites from Cannon's Point Plantation
         (1794-1861), St. Simon's Island, Georgia." Ph.D dissertation, Univer-
         sity of Florida.

Palmer, Arlene
  1976   A Winterthur Guide to Chinese Export Porcelain. Crown Publishers,
         New York.

Prime, Alfred Coxe
  1929   The Arts and Crafts in Philadelphia, Maryland and South Carolina,
         Part I. 1721-1785: Gleanings from Newspapers. The Walpole Society.
         Reprinted by Da Capo Press, New York, 1969.

  1932   The Arts and Crafts in Philadelphia, Maryland and South Carolina,
         Part II. 1786-1800: Gleanings from Newspapers. The Walpole Society.
         Reprinted by Da Capo Press, New York, 1969.

Quimby, Ian M. G., ed.
  1973   Ceramics in America. The University Press of Virginia, Charlottesville,
         Va.

216

Roth, Rodris
1961 "Tea Drinking in 18th-Century America: Its Etiquette and Equipage."
      Contributions from the Museum of History and Technology, Paper 14.
      Smithsonian Institution, Washington, D.C.

Rust, Gordon A.
1973 Collector's Guide to Antique Porcelain. Viking Press, New York.

Shaw, Simeon
1829 History of the Staffordshire Potteries; and the Rise and Progress of
      the Manufacture of Pottery and Porcelain. Reprint. Great Neck, N.Y.,
      1968.

Simmons, Harold C.
1969 Archaeological Photography. New York University Press, New York.

Smith, Robin L., and Honerkamp, Nicholas
1976 "An Archeological Assessment of the Cultural Resources at Mulberry
      Grove Plantation, Chatham County, Georgia." Report on file at
      University of Florida.

South, Stanley
1972 "Evolution and Horizon as Revealed in Ceramic Analysis in Historical
      Archaeology." The Conference on Historic Site Archaeology Papers, 1971,
      6:71-116.
1974 "Palmetto Parapets: Exploratory Archeology at Fort Moultrie, South
      Carolina, 38CH50." Anthropological Studies #1, Occasional Papers of
      the Institute of Archeology and Anthropology. University of South
      Carolina, Columbia, S.C.

1977 Method and Theory in Historical Archeology. Academic Press, New York.

Stone, Garry Wheeler
1970 "Ceramics in Suffolk County, Massachusetts Inventories 1680-1775: A
      Preliminary Study with Divers Comments Thereon, and Sundry Suggestions."
      The Conference on Historic Site Archaeology Papers, 1968, 3:73-90.

Watkins, Lura Woodside
1950 Early New England Potters and Their Wares. Harvard University Press,
      Cambridge, Mass.

PERSONAL COMMUNICATION

Chase, Charles E., historical architect, Drayton Hall Project, National
  Trust for Historic Preservation.

Fairbanks, Charles H., chairman, Department of Anthropology, University of
  Florida.

Hastie, Norwood, former owner and director, Magnolia Gardens, Charleston, S.C.
  (Drayton descendant).

Murphy, Kevin, architectural historian, Drayton Hall Project, National Trust
for Historic Preservation.

Noel Hume, Ivor, chief archaeologist, Colonial Williamsburg.

Palmer, Arlene, curator of ceramics and glass, Winterthur Museum, Winterthur, Del.

Wardell, Jean, president, South Carolina Historical Society, Charleston, S.C.